College English
Self-adaptive Reading

新指南大学英语
自主阅读 ①

总主编　李华东

主　编　耿艳萍

副主编　娄媛媛　诸葛晓初

编　者　王　怡　陈正正　王天真

　　　　杨愫愫　张　帆　李温榕

　　　　白鹤鸣　董　倩　朱莉雅

清华大学出版社

北　京

内 容 简 介

《新指南大学英语自主阅读》1—4册是根据教育部最新发布的《大学英语教学指南（2020版）》，为我国普通高等院校大学生量身打造的一套自主阅读教材。

本套书每册包括8个单元，每个单元包含视频导入、语言输入、阅读技巧和语言输出4大部分：导入部分精选主题相关视频，扫码即看，并设计有理解性和思辨性练习；语言输入部分由Banked Cloze、Long Passage和 Short Passages 3个板块组成，所选篇章均借助语言数据技术，标注了篇章长度（NW）、语言难度（GL）、语言学术性（AWL percentage）和关键词（Keywords）等数据，练习与大学英语四、六级考试题型完全接轨；1—4册共32个单元的阅读技巧板块有机融入，构成完整的阅读技能训练体系；语言输出部分聚焦学术词汇训练和写作训练。

本套教材兼顾基础级别目标（第1、2册）和提高级别目标（第3、4册），适合我国普通高校一、二年级大学生使用。

图书在版编目（CIP）数据

新指南大学英语自主阅读.1 / 李华东总主编；耿艳萍主编. — 北京：清华大学出版社，2021.7（2024.8重印）

ISBN 978-7-302-58459-9

Ⅰ.①新… Ⅱ.①李…②耿… Ⅲ.①英语－阅读教学－高等学校－教材 Ⅳ.①H319.37

中国版本图书馆CIP数据核字(2021)第118462号

责任编辑：刘细珍
封面设计：子　一
责任校对：王凤芝
责任印制：丛怀宇

出版发行：清华大学出版社
　　　　网　　址：https://www.tup.com.cn, https://www.wqxuetang.com
　　　　地　　址：北京清华大学学研大厦 A 座　　　邮　编：100084
　　　　社 总 机：010-83470000　　　邮　购：010-62786544
　　　　投稿与读者服务：010-62776969, c-service@tup.tsinghua.edu.cn
　　　　质 量 反 馈：010-62772015, zhiliang@tup.tsinghua.edu.cn
印 装 者：三河市铭诚印务有限公司
经　　销：全国新华书店
开　　本：185mm×260mm　　印　张：11.5　　字　数：212千字
版　　次：2021 年 7 月第 1 版　　印　次：2024 年 8 月第 8 次印刷
定　　价：56.00 元

产品编号：092133-02

《新指南大学英语自主阅读》是根据教育部最新发布的《大学英语教学指南（2020版）》（以下简称"《指南》"），借助语言数据技术，为我国普通高等院校大学生量身定制的一套自主阅读教材。

一、教材特色

本套教材务求体现以下特色：

1. 依据《指南》编写，针对基础和提高级别

《指南》指出，"大学英语教学目标分为基础、提高、发展三个级别"，并对三个级别的阅读理解能力进行了描述。本套教材针对基础和提高两个级别研发，能覆盖绝大多数普通高等院校大学生，满足他们提高英语阅读理解能力的需求。

2. 借助语言数据技术，助力自主阅读

为帮助学习者了解自己的水平，掌控自己的阅读进度，本套教材所选阅读篇章均标注了篇章语言数据，具体如下：

- 篇章长度（number of words，简称"NW"）：便于自学者了解自己的阅读速度（速度 = 篇章长度 / 阅读时间）。

- 语言难度（Flesch-Kincaid Grade Level，简称"GL"）：GL 数值等于美国学生年级，比如 GL 为 8 的篇章从难度上适合美国八年级学生阅读。近10 年来我国主要英语考试的英语阅读篇章 GL 数值分别为：高考英语 8.3左右，大学英语四级考试 10.8 左右，大学英语六级考试 11.8 左右。

- 语言学术性（Academic Word List percentage，简称"AWL percentage"）：采用 Coxhead 于 2000 年研发的学术词表，计算每篇阅读中学术词汇比例，便于自学者提高自身学术英语阅读能力。依据 Coxhead 的研究，学术语篇的AWL percentage 比例为 9.9% 左右。

- 关键词（keywords）：每篇文章提供 3 个关键词，便于自学者在阅读前大致了解文章内容。

按照克拉申（Krashen）的输入假设（Input Hypothesis），制约语言习得的

主要因素是语言输入，而最佳的语言输入是稍稍超出学习者现有语言能力的输入。借助上述语言数据，自学者可以了解自己的阅读水平和阅读喜好，从而选择稍稍超出自己现有阅读水平的篇章进行阅读，进而有针对性地提高自己的语言能力。

3. 实施主题教学模式，提高词汇复现率

本套教材选择与中国大学生学习和生活密切相关的话题，每个单元围绕同一个话题展开，在加大学习者知识广度和深度的同时，提高词汇复现率，并穿插视频观看（Viewing）和写作（Writing）环节，有效将学生的认知性词汇（passive vocabulary）转化为复用式词汇（active vocabulary）。

二、教材架构

本套教材包括 4 册书，书后均附视频脚本和练习参考答案。每册主题和语言技能安排如下表：

级别	主题	阅读技能设置
1	大学生活、教育、时尚、饮食、情感、旅行、性格、社交	以《指南》规定的基础级别目标阅读技能为主
2	爱情、成长、大学校园文化、生活方式、感情与交往、合作与冲突、创业、职业规划	
3	课外生活、语言的力量、健康与美容、跨文化交际、数据时代、创新、人工智能、基因技术	以《指南》规定的提高级别目标阅读技能为主
4	职业规划、工作选择、财务管理、旅行、环保、因特网与生活、工作地点选择、新教育模式	

三、单元设置

本套教材每册包括 8 个单元，每个单元包含 4 大部分共 7 个板块，其中语言输入部分的练习形式采用大学英语四、六级考试的 4 种题型，具有极强的针对性。具体单元设置如下表：

模块构思	板块设置	板块描述
导入	Viewing（视频导入）	通过与单元主题相关的精选视频导入本单元的主题，引发学生阅读兴趣

语言输入	Banked Cloze（集库式完形填空）	以集库式完形填空形式拓展学生的词汇量和语篇理解能力
	Long Passage（长篇速读）	以信息匹配形式提高学生的快速阅读（skimming and scanning）能力
	Short Passages（短篇细读）	通过多项选择题（multi-choice questions），全面提高学生的阅读理解能力，如掌握主旨（main idea）、找寻细节（details）、进行推断（inference）、词语释义（paraphrase）、判断态度（attitude）等能力
阅读技巧训练	Reading Skills（阅读技巧训练）	根据本单元阅读篇章特点，总结阅读技巧，并进行适度拓展练习，训练学生掌握这些阅读技巧
语言输出	Academic Words in Use（学术词汇训练）	精选本单元出现过的学术词汇，以集库式完形填空形式训练学生，让他们学会使用这些学术词汇，提高学生学术阅读能力，能用英语作为媒介学习学术内容
	Writing（写作训练）	通过写作训练复习本单元所学内容。训练题型有三种：一是大学英语四、六级考试作文题型；二是读后续写；三是单元内容小结

四、适用对象

本套教材适合我国普通高校一、二年级大学生使用，兼顾基础级别目标（第1、2 册）和提高级别目标（第 3、4 册），并适度关注了学术词汇的学习。

五、教材使用建议

本套教材主要用于学生课下自学，可以与大学英语主干教材配套使用，也可以单独使用。

六、编写团队

本套教材总主编为上海海事大学李华东教授，第 1—4 册分别由温州商学院、内蒙古大学、浙江传媒学院和上海政法学院的教研团队编写。丛书编写方案由上海海事大学团队研发，主要成员包括朱莉雅、刘慧丹、陈园园、郝韵涵等。感谢清华大学出版社刘细珍老师在丛书策划、编写和成书过程中给予的大力支持。

本套教材系国家社会科学基金项目（17BYY103）部分成果。

由于编写时间紧，本套教材可能存在错漏和不妥之处，请教材使用者批评指正。

《新指南大学英语自主阅读》编写团队

2021 年 5 月

Contents

Contents

Unit 1 A Brand-New Start

Viewing

Welcome to Stanford

About the video clip

This video introduces the campus life at Stanford University. While enjoying the campus tour at Stanford, do you still remember the very first impression of your campus?

Understanding the clip

Below are some statements that are mentioned in the video clip. Decide whether these statements are true or false. Write T if the statements are true, or F if the statements are false, or NG (Not Given) if the statements are not mentioned in the video clip. Answer the questions by ticking (√) the corresponding letter.

	T	F	NG
1. The first student was jittery and nervous when he was a freshman coming to Stanford.	☐	☐	☐
2. The second student was scared about preparing for a speech at student orientation.	☐	☐	☐
3. Orientation begins the year at Stanford and bonds students as a class.	☐	☐	☐
4. Meeting upperclassmen is important because they will become your best friend.	☐	☐	☐

5. The great part about orientation is everyone getting settled in his/her dorm. ☐ ☐ ☐

6. Students are encouraged to embrace the perfection and imperfection at Stanford. ☐ ☐ ☐

Further thoughts

As a freshman, you certainly expect a lot from your campus life. Meanwhile, you may experience nervousness. Could you please list some of your expectations in the table below?

Expectations	Nervousness
1. Making new friends.	1. Dorm life.
2. Joining a variety of associations.	2. Building a community.

Banked Cloze

Below is a passage with ten blanks. You are required to select one word for each blank from the list of choices given in a word bank following the passage. Read the passage carefully before making your choices. Each choice in the blank is identified by a letter. Please write the corresponding letter for each item in the blanks. You may not use any of the words in the bank more than once.

Tips to Help You to Excel at College[1]

NW: 252 GL: 7.2 AWL percentage: 3.91% Keywords: studies; problems; lifestyle

There are some key factors you need to keep in mind when you are at college if you want to do well.

Firstly, always put your studies first. Some students quickly fall into the 1._____ of putting their social life in front of their studies, and this is the start of a slippery slope. While you may find you suddenly have lots of new friends and 2._____ social event invitations, you have to focus on your studies above all else. Keep focusing on the reason why you are at college and think about the huge impact your college 3._____ will have on your future.

---

1 From Mid Hudson News website.

4._____, make sure you tackle problems. As a student, you are 5._____ to have problems with your studies now and again. For example, you could find yourself stuck on a particular homework or you may struggle with a(n) 6._____ subject. You can tackle them by getting help online, or you can also speak to your tutor about getting some more help or support.

Last but not least, keep a healthy lifestyle. Many students fail to realize the importance of keeping a healthy lifestyle while at college. Many fail to eat 7._____, turning to fast food for convenience or even 8._____ meals altogether. Things like sleep and diet are very important, as they 9._____ your ability to focus on your studies. So, make sure you live a healthy life at college.

To 10._____, these are some of the key things that can help you to enjoy far greater success when you are at college.

A) exciting	B) grades	C) specific
D) particularly	E) conclude	F) bound
G) skipping	H) dietary	I) trap
J) summary	K) affect	L) future
M) furthermore	N) healthily	O) growing

Long Passage

You are going to read a passage with ten statements attached to it. Each statement contains information given in one of the paragraphs. Identify the paragraph from which the information is derived. You may choose a paragraph more than once. Each paragraph is marked with a letter. Please answer the questions by writing the corresponding letter after the statements.

College Orientation for Students and Parents[2]

NW: 978 GL: 9 **AWL percentage:** 3.79% **Keywords:** orientation; freshman; prepare

A   College orientation for freshmen is a way for students to meet other students and become familiar with all campus services. While orientation has been generally for students, in the last 10 years, colleges have recognized the fact that parents need help dealing with the change. So, they have added parent orientation.

B   Student orientation will be your first real college experience. Even if you've visited the campus in the past, it will be the first time you go there as an official student. For many schools, like Texas A&M's Fish Camp, orientation is mandatory. But even if it's not, you

---

2 From Teenlife website.

should make plans to attend.

C   You can certainly attend orientation expecting to learn what you need to know there, but it's helpful to do some research beforehand. Read all the information the college sends you. Bring any paperwork you will need such as vaccination records.

D   Many colleges also have you sign up for classes while at orientation. Look at the course catalog as it pertains to your study. You will get an idea of the classes you need to take and electives you could choose. Advisors will be there to help, so it will make it easier.

E   The most important thing at orientation is to get acquainted with college life. You will attend "getting to know you" sessions, informational sessions, and advising sessions. During the evening, most colleges offer fun activities like parties, sport competitions and games. Orientation gives you the opportunity to make friends, get acquainted with roommates, buy textbooks, and become comfortable with navigating the campus.

F   Colleges provide incoming freshmen with information about the different clubs and organizations on campus. It's a great opportunity to learn about each one and determine what you would like to take part in. Whether you want to be part of a service organization, play intramural sports, be active politically, write for the campus paper, work at the campus radio station, this is the time to get information on each.

G   If the college has Greek life, orientation will probably have some informal rush activities and you will be able to speak with representatives from the sorority and/or fraternity. This is a good way to decide if Greek life is right for you and which groups you feel comfortable with. Sign up for email of any club or organization you're remotely interested in, ask for contact information from representatives, ask about the organization's social media presence as well.

H   Doing this helps you stay in the loop and make a decision once your arrive on campus. It'd be better to stay overnight in the dorms instead of staying overnight with your parents. This is the best way to immerse yourself in campus life and get to know other students. You may not make lifelong friends at orientation, but you should still socialize with as many people as possible. Remember that everyone is in the same boat— they are just as new as you are and probably just as nervous. Try starting a conversation in the dining hall with someone you have never met. Come and join in all the social activities provided by the orientation leaders. This will help you get to know one another. Once you are out socializing, talk to lots of people instead of just clinging to one person.

I   Parents may experience this education moment as a relief, a cause for worry, or both; and many would like a little guidance. College orientation for parents can provide some of that guidance, as well as equipping parents with a more accurate mental picture of what their child's new life will be like.

J   College orientation offers students and parents a glimpse of the school and the campus. It's very important in the whole family's life for the next four years for both parents and students. Becoming familiar with the campus and the school will make it easier for parents to understand their children's lives and have informed conversations with them in the coming years. Learning about school rules and campus safety will also be of practical value to many parents. Meeting other parents will also provide a feeling of community, as well as the potential for long-lasting friendships.

K   Try to think of yourself as both a parent and a student during your orientation. Bring paper and pencil or an iPad to take notes with, make sure to ask questions and introduce yourself to parents and school officials. Especially at a large college, it can be helpful to get to know some contacts personally or at least to know who to talk to if you have a question about financial aid or your child's academic record. In addition to taking care of the practical details, you will also enjoy it.

L   In recent years, more and more colleges and universities have offered orientation events especially geared toward parents during the days, weeks, or months before school starts. The Boston Globe reports that most parents found the events to be more than worthwhile. With events starting from "Meet the Dean" to model classes and seminars on "Letting Go", parent orientations offer an in-depth understanding of today's college experience. Colleges also offer sessions on student health, campus safety, Q&A sessions and so on.

M   It's clear that orientation is the first college activity that students (and parents) should attend. Parents, remember to maintain your boundaries and ask questions to ease your mind. Students, don't forget to embrace this new experience by taking advantage of it.

1. Freshmen can register for classes and get to know course catalog at orientation. ☐

2. There are many sessions and fun activities for freshmen to attend at orientation. ☐

3. One of the best way to get to know other students is to stay overnight in the dorm. ☐

4. Freshmen and their parents learn about school rules and campus safety at orientation. ☐

5. Orientation for freshmen is a good way to become familiar with everything on campus. ☐

6. Freshmen should attend orientation as this is students' very first real college experience. ☐

7. It's a great opportunity to get to know many different clubs and organizations at orientation. ☐

8. Orientation provides guidance for parents and presents a mental picture of their child's new life at college. ☐

9. Freshmen can take part in some activities at orientation to see if Greek life is right for them. ☐

10. Colleges offer orientation events for both freshmen and their parents before semester starts. ☐

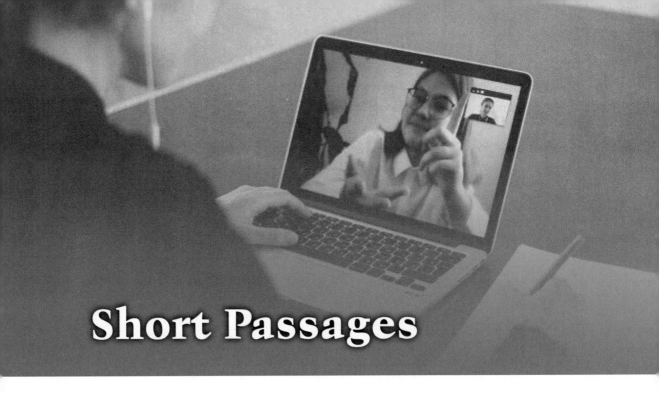

Short Passages

There are 2 passages in this part. Each passage is followed by some questions or unfinished statements. After each passage, there are four choices marked A, B, C, and D. You should decide on the best choice and mark the corresponding letter.

Passage one

Stanford University Students Flock to a Virtual Campus[3]

NW: 360 GL: 9 AWL percentage: 3.8% Keywords: platform; website; virtual campus

Stanford students, facing a new semester of remote learning, have come up with a novel way of coping: they've invented "Club Cardinal", a gamified virtual campus. It is a new digital platform that allows students to explore campus and connect in Zoom rooms during the school's COVID-19 shutdown.

Club Cardinal is a free website that looks like a game of "the Farm", Stanford campus's nickname. Students use a stanford.edu email address to choose avatars and receive dorm

---

3 From Smithsonian Magazine website.

rooms. They can decorate with furniture and other things from a virtual store. Students can explore the virtual Stanford campus via a map featuring campus landmarks, such as the Oval, Meyer Green, Main Quad, Green Library and the late-night eatery known as TAP. Each place has its own Zoom room for video chatting with other users whose avatars are nearby. Club Cardinal users accumulate money for decorating dorms by spending time on the platform and can store those savings in a virtual bank.

The club was launched on August 1st. It has a calendar system to let users know about virtual events. Student groups can host gatherings via Zoom in virtual places. There are "coffee chats" with faculty members, informational sessions with a capella groups, "ask an upperclassman" Q&As, and even class reunions. The club recently held a "virtual activity" fair with some 40 student groups. As of late August, there were 3,000 users (Stanford has about 7,000 undergraduates). Faculty members are encouraged to join Club Cardinal as well. Their avatars have red name tags.

Students have hosted birthday parties, gone virtual "fountain hopping" (a tradition on the campus dotted with 25 fountains), played tag, organized races and had long chats with old friends. The class reunions, for both alumni and current students, have been especially popular.

It is hoped that Club Cardinal, in the long term, will be developed into a social platform. Students from many different colleges can visit each other's campus. They can hold events on a central platform, and connect all within the visual appeal of a virtual world.

1. **What does the underlined word "semester" (Line 1, Para. 1) mean?**

   A. Term.

   B. Course

   C. Subject.

   D. Curriculum.

2. **What can we learn about Club Cardinal mentioned by the author?**

   A. Club Cardinal is the creator of gamified virtual campus.

   B. Club Cardinal is a free website for Stanford students.

   C. Club Cardinal offers a nickname for Stanford campus.

   D. Club Cardinal is a platform for students to copy everything.

3. **What can Stanford students do with the virtual campus?**

A. Students can store savings in their dorm rooms.

B. Students can decorate a virtual store on campus.

C. Students can explore the Green Library via a map.

D. Students can video chat with others in a virtual bank.

4. **Which statement is true about the "virtual activity" fair?**

A. Stanford students' avatars have red name tags.

B. It was first launched on August 1st at Stanford University.

C. There were 3,000 faculty members joining the virtual activity.

D. There were approximately 40 student groups joining the fair.

5. **What can we infer from the passage?**

A. Stanford students hope to host birthday parties in the real life.

B. The purpose of the club's calendar system is to launch virtual events.

C. The class reunions are very popular among the 7,000 undergraduates.

D. Club Cardinal may expand itself beyond Stanford campus.

Passage two

On-campus Life of Freshmen[4]

NW: 358 GL: 7.7 AWL percentage: 3.76% Keywords: freshmen; campus life; activities

Welcome, freshmen! Soon you'll leave the comforts of home for dorm showers, dining hall meals, and long walks to classes—and it's going to be great. Here's some advice from a former freshman on how to live your best (on-campus) life.

First of all, let's start with a priority: food. There are canteens in each of the main on-campus living areas. My main advice is to try them all, as they each bring something different to the table.

---

4 From Onward State website.

Next, good luck putting off the inevitable, but you'll eventually have to study. Though some students opt to study in the dorms, there are plenty of spots on campus to get work done. The Pattee and the Paterno Libraries are where you'll find most students working, ranging from the quiet stacks to the reading room, which is more affectionately known as the Harry Potter room.

When it comes to leisurely activities, you'll have many choices. First, the involvement fair. There are over 1,000 organizations at University Park that you can join, so check out all the organizations at University Park here. In addition, the Student Programming Association, or SPA, hosts weekly LateNight at the HUB, as well as tons of free concerts and lectures. Participants can expect to watch movies and attend the occasional comedy shows. The timetable can be found online as well. Lastly, the gyms and outdoor facilities on campus are available and you should definitely take advantage of them, as they're now included in your student fee, so membership is "free". There are also volleyball, tennis, and basketball courts, which are the perfect spots for hanging out on a warm day.

Last but not least, there is something really important about transportation you need to know. As the temperature drops and the wind picks up, you'll want to figure out your ideal bus route! The White Loop, or Whoop, travels counterclockwise around campus and through downtown, while the Blue Loop, or Bloop, travels in the clockwise direction. Luckily, these CATA buses are free, so don't worry about needing to carry around change to hitch a ride.

1. **What is the tone of Paragraph 1?**

A. Jokey.

B. Authoritative.

C. Serious.

D. Friendly.

2. **What can we learn from Paragraph 2?**

A. Students have to study and eventually get work done only in their dorms.

B. There are places for students to enjoy meals in the on-campus living areas.

C. The two laboratories available to students are the Pattee and the Paterno.

D. There is a Harry Potter's reading room which is affectionately known to students.

3. **Which statement is true about leisurely activities?**

A. Only freshmen can join the involvement fair.

B. SPA hosts LateNight concerts and lectures at University Park.

C. The timetable for movies and comedy shows can be found online.

D. Students must take advantage of the gyms because of the free membership.

4. **Why do students need to know about the transportation?**

A. Because it's necessary for students to figure out the ideal bus route.

B. Because the White Loop goes clockwise around campus.

C. Because the Blue Loop goes counterclockwise around campus.

D. Because students often need to carry around change to catch a bus.

5. **What does the underlined phrase "picks up" (Line 2, Para. 5) mean?**

A. Eases up.

B. Sinks down.

C. Tails off.

D. Springs up.

Reading Skills

Skimming and Scanning

1 How to skim

The aim of skimming a text is to grasp a brief idea or get an overview of a text in order to get the meaning of the text quickly. Useful tips for better skimming:

1. Read the title, subtitles or subheading;
2. Look at the illustrations;
3. Read the first and last sentence of each paragraph;
4. Take in keywords;
5. Grasp the main ideas.

2 How to scan

The aim of scanning a text is to read for specific details. Useful tips for better scanning:

1. Don't try to read every word;
2. Use clues on the page, such as headings and titles;
3. Use the "header" words to help you;

4. Think up or write down some questions;

5. Many texts use A-Z order;

6. There are many ways to practice scanning skills.

Exercises

Please read the above reading skills of skimming and scanning. Use the means for the following paragraphs.

Paragraph 1

College orientation for freshmen is a way for students to meet other students and become familiar with all campus services. While orientation has been generally for students, in the last 10 years, colleges have recognized the fact that parents need help dealing with the change. So, they have added parent orientation.

Skim Paragraph 1 and grasp keywords: _____

Paragraph 2

When it comes to leisurely activities, you'll have many choices. First, the involvement fair. There are over 1,000 organizations at University Park that you can join, so check out all the organizations at University Park here. In addition, the Student Programming Association, or SPA, hosts weekly LateNight at the HUB, as well as tons of free concerts and lectures. Participants can expect to watch movies, and attend the occasional comedy shows. The timetable can be found online as well. Lastly, the gyms and outdoor facilities on campus are available and you should definitely take advantage of them, as they're now included in your student fee, so membership is "free". There are also volleyball, tennis, and basketball courts, which are the perfect spots for hanging out on a warm day.

Skim Paragraph 2 and grasp the main idea: _____

Paragraph 3

The most important thing at orientation is to get acquainted with college life. You will attend "getting to know you" sessions, informational sessions, and advising sessions. During the evening, most colleges offer fun activities like parties, sport competitions and games. Orientation gives you the opportunity to make friends, get acquainted with roommates, buy textbooks, and become comfortable with navigating the campus.

Scan Paragraph 3 and answer the question: What are the things you may get acquainted with college life? _____

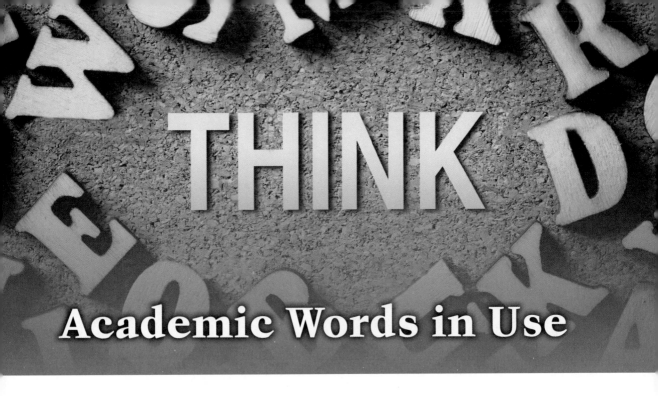

THINK

Academic Words in Use

Fill in the blanks in the following sentences with the appropriate words provided in the box below. Change the form of the words if necessary.

leisurely	community	facility	eventually	lecture	via
mental	maintain	focus	affectionately	accurate	virtual

1. We exited _____ a fire door.

2. We walked _____ into the hotel.

3. The house is large and difficult to _____.

4. The figure is _____ to two decimal places.

5. It was a long journey, but we _____ arrived.

6. It was the main _____ of attention at the meeting.

7. She gave Tom a big smile and hugged him _____.

8. You may wish to take advantage of our instructional _____.

9. Many people suffer from _____ illness at some point in their lives.

10. New technology has enabled development of an online "_____ library".

11. These _____ are open to both undergraduate and post-graduate students.

12. The school has established a successful relationship with the local _____.

Writing

For this part, you are allowed 30 minutes to write a short essay entitled "How to Succeed in College". You should write at least 120 words but no more than 180 words.

How to Succeed in College

Unit **2** College Education: East and West

Viewing

How the American Colleges Lift Students Out of Poverty

About the video clip

This video clip discusses how the American colleges work at lifting students out of poverty.

Understanding the video clip

The bottom 20% are the families making about $25,000 or less per year. The economists looked at the college they went to and how their position on the income ladder changed after their graduation. Watch the video clip and fill in the blanks in the table below.

Colleges	Data	Results
Harvard	Over _____ of them go from families in the poorest fifth of the American economy, to being in the top _____ by the time they're in their mid-thirties. In the class of 2013 only _____ of Harvard students came from the bottom 20% of the income distribution.	The kids who go to _____ colleges do really well, but plenty of qualified low income students are not _____ to these school.

Moultrie Technical College	_____ of their students came from the bottom rung of the ladder.	It's really good at _____, but a very small fraction of them make it to the top fifth of the income _____.
Cal State LA	_____ of students come from the bottom rung of the ladder and _____ of them end up at the top rung.	David Leonhardt at *The New York Times* refers to them as America's Great _____ Colleges. They are not the famous ones but they're doing the work.
PACE University	_____ of its students come from the bottom rung of the ladder, but well over _____ of them wind up in the top 20%.	

Further thoughts

As the investigation shows, those who get access to elite universities, such as Harvard and Stanford, are more likely to come from wealthy families. Do you think "impoverished families can hardly nurture rich sons"? List evidence in the table below to support each argument.

Yes	No
1. Low income families cannot afford tuition of those elite universities.	1. Funding and students loans can reduce the financial burden of impoverished families.
2. Students from wealthy families have privilege for better educational resources.	2. Students from poor families have more motivation to work hard and change life.

Banked Cloze

Below is a passage with ten blanks. You are required to select one word for each blank from the list of choices given in a word bank following the passage. Read the passage carefully before making your choices. Each choice in the bank is identified by a letter. Please write the corresponding letter for each item in the blanks. You may not use any of the words in the bank more than once.

Grading Grades in the US Colleges[1]

NW: 311 GL: 8.5 AWL percentage: 6.9% Keywords: program; evergreen; grade

A small number of colleges—perhaps about twenty nationally—refuse the traditional grading system of A, B, C, D and F. The Evergreen State College, for example, was 1.____ in 1967 and has never used letter or number grades. Evergreen State is a(n) 2.____ four-year college in the northwestern city of Olympia, Washington. It has more than four thousand students, including twenty-six international students 3.____. Evergreen State is organized into programs taught by groups of professors. Each program brings together 4.____ subjects and extends in length over two or three quarters. Students are 5.____ to do a main research project at the end of each program. The professors write detailed evaluations of the students. These are 6.____ with evaluations written by the

---

1 From VOA website.

students themselves. Students also meet with their professors to 7._____ their work. The director of admissions, Doug Scrima, says employers and graduate schools like these evaluations. He says they show more about the 8._____ of students' work than traditional grades do.

Alverno College in Milwaukee, Wisconsin is a small women's school that does not use grades. Kathleen O'Brien is the chief academic officer. She says letter grades do not 9._____ document learning or provide good direction to students. But she says the American university system is not organized to accept this kind of 10._____.

A) currently	B) demanded	C) deserted
D) founded	E) effectively	F) discuss
G) public	H) deliberately	I) habit
J) combined	K) quality	L) enough
M) change	N) avoid	O) different

Long Passage

You are going to read a passage with ten statements attached to it. Each statement contains information given in one of the paragraphs. Identify the paragraph from which the information is derived. You may choose a paragraph more than once. Each paragraph is marked with a letter. Please answer the questions by writing the corresponding letter after the statements.

Double Major in University[2]

NW: 1,034 GL: 9.4 AWL percentage: 7.6% Keywords: double; major; elective

A   In university, you use a credit system in order to earn a degree. Upon completing a class successfully, you'll earn a determined number of credits towards your final degree. When doing a double major, a student has completed enough credits from two different programs or disciplines. By contrast, most students will opt to focus on one major and then fill in the rest of their credits with some minor or elective classes. However, it's important to understand that students who do a double major still only graduate with one degree.

B   The reasons for doing a double major vary from student to student. Sometimes

---

2 From University of People website.

the reasons are personal, such as an interest in two subjects, while sometimes they're strategic or for professional purposes. That being said, there are some key reasons why you might consider doing a double major. Here are a few of them:

C   Expand your career choices. Sometimes, the fields in which students choose to do a double major can be intrinsically or even loosely related. For example, a degree in both Business and Foreign Languages can help improve your employment chances internationally. A double major in both Arts and Marketing can help you understand and monetize the business side to a creative field. Aside from just opening the door to more careers, it can also be helpful to double major if you plan on applying to graduate school. If you have a set direction for your education and you already know the requirements for competitive graduate schools, a double major can help you become a better candidate for a specialized graduate program.

D   Stand out from the rest. In 2015, only about 12% of undergraduate college students had a double major. Since double major students are still in the minority, graduating with a double major can help you stand out from others in your field. Imagine everyone in your major graduates applies for the same pool of works. How would an employer differentiate between the candidates? If a candidate completed a double major with a second degree in a related or interesting field, it can really help them get a leg up.

E   Get the most out of your tuition. One of the most practical reasons for doing a double major is simply getting more out of your college years and tuition fee. While your university may charge you by credit or credit hours, it's still worth taking on the relatively small cost to maximize your education. As you know most of your other costs such as student housing and transportation will remain the same. Doing a double major is a better option in the long run compared to going back to school for a second degree.

F   While some students see the advantages of a double major, others would rather spend their time and energy towards a dual degree. The main difference is that with a double major, you graduate with one degree, while with a dual or double degree, you would finish school with two completely separate degrees. Furthermore, some schools offer joint programs where you can complete a first degree and an advanced degree simultaneously, such as a B.A. and M.A. While a dual degree seems like a more favorable option, you should know it usually comes at a higher cost and takes more time to complete. It's also important to consider that you need to apply to two separate programs, so you need to make sure you have the prerequisites for both.

G   With the right mindset and enough strategic planning, doing a double major is definitely manageable. Here are a few important tips to consider before you decide to pursue a double major:

H   Make a plan. Starting a double major shouldn't be a decision you take lightly. It requires a certain amount of planning in advance. You don't necessarily need to begin your second major in your first semester. It is a good idea to start tackling both course loads earlier in your degree so that you have enough time to focus on your courses without being rushed. More importantly, planning in advance is necessary since it will help you consider if you're really committed to doing a double major, or if you're simply unsure of what field you'd like to study.

I   If you've decided to go ahead with a double major, then choosing the right courses is an important element for success. See if you can find classes that are related to your two majors so that you can make your credits count for both. You also want to avoid overlap so that you're not working harder than you need to. Finally, use your electives wisely. Often, a major will come with a certain number of elective credits you need to complete, so these can often be put towards your second major. Hence, you should be strategic in your course choices.

J   Consider staying an extra semester. There's absolutely no shame in extending your degree by an extra semester or two if you think it's the best option for your education. If you're OK with having a full course load every semester, then you can probably complete your degree in four years. However, if you know that you'll need more time to study for two majors, or to work part-time, it might be in your best interest to take an extra semester.

K   Additionally, you can consistently remind yourself why you've decided to take on a double major. Doing a double major can be hard, and you might find yourself overworked or stressed sometimes, especially during exam periods. Take a step back and assess why you've decided to do a double major. Are you working towards your dream career? Are you exploring two of your passions? Simply adding a second major for the sake of adding it to your CV may not be the best reason to overwork yourself. Make sure to check in with yourself frequently, reassess your reasons, and keep looking towards your goal.

1. A student needs to work out a plan before doing a double major. ☐

2. Doing a double major tends to be more economical compared to returning to college for a second degree. ☐

3. Double major students could be more advantaged when they apply for graduate schools. ☐

4. Some students may strain themselves from time to time while taking a second major. ☐

5. The differences between a double major and a double degree program could be seen easily. ☐

6. Different students have different reasons for doing a double major at university. ☐

7. A graduate with a double major tends to outshine others in the job market. ☐

8. If necessary, a student can prolong the time at university for doing a double major. ☐

9. Students need to be strategic in choosing the courses for doing a double major. ☐

10. Double major students may feel exhausted during exam periods. ☐

Short Passages

There are 2 passages in this module. Each passage is followed by some questions or unfinished statements. For each passage there are four choices marked A, B, C, and D. You should decide on the best choice and mark the corresponding letter.

Passage one

What Is EAP?[3]

NW: 375 GL: 9.5 **AWL percentage:** 4.35% **Keywords:** lecture; English; academic

The object of an EAP (English for Academic Purposes) course is to help foreign students overcome some of the linguistic difficulties in studying in English. The job of the EAP lecturer is to find out what the students have to do and help them to do it better. EAP students are usually current higher education students or they are hoping to go on to higher education after their EAP course. They need to learn English in order to succeed in their academic careers.

Most universities in the UK offer these pre-sessional courses, which vary in length from one year to two weeks. The EAP courses often take place at the institution where the students intend to take their main academic course but this needs not be the case.

---

3 From What Is EAP website.

These courses are intended to prepare students in higher education coming to study in the UK to study in English. They also allow students to familiarize themselves with the new environment and facilities of the schools before their main courses start. The students need to learn to adopt particular approaches to their study and learn skills that will support them to succeed in the UK HE system. The purpose of the pre-sessional EAP course is to bring them up to the level that is necessary to start a course. In this case EAP tutors need to liaise with admissions tutors to find out what is necessary.

EAP courses can also be in-sessional courses. That is they are taken at the same time as the students' main academic course. In-sessional courses can take one of two forms. They can be seen as language support classes—these are usually free drop-in classes held at lunch-times or Wednesday afternoons and students attend when they are able. Increasingly it is also becoming possible for international students to take credit-bearing EAP courses as part of their degree.

Most EAP lecturers are involved to some extent in testing students in higher education. This advises admissions tutors on what external English language tests are available and what the scores mean. On the basis of these scores, students can be accepted or given offers conditionally on reaching a particular level of English. Or they need to attend a certain length pre-sessional course.

1. Who are EAP students?

A. They are foreign students whose main course will be English.

B. They are foreign students currently taking higher education in the UK.

C. They are foreign students who have to advance English for their careers.

D. They are foreign students with language obstacles when they study in English.

2. What can we learn about EAP courses?

A. EAP courses normally last for two weeks or one year.

B. EAP courses only improve students' language proficiency.

C. EAP courses help students adapt to their new schools' environment.

D. EAP courses take place at the institution where students have main course.

3. What does the underlined word "liaise" (Line 10, Para. 2) mean?

A. Compete.

B. Review.

C. Communicate.

D. Greet.

4. What can we infer from the third paragraph?

A. In-sessional EAP courses do not have flexible time slots.

B. Extra language lessons are normally scheduled in the evenings.

C. Students take in-sessional EAP courses although they cannot get credits.

D. Students may not have main course arranged on Wednesday afternoons.

5. What do admissions tutors need to do involved to EAP courses?

A. They need to help students learn English to succeed in UK HE system.

B. They need to provide students with learning skills ahead of main course.

C. They need to inform students of English language tests required for application.

D. They need to give applicants language examinations to test their English level.

Passage two

Westlake University[4]

NW: 327 GL: 8.8 AWL percentage: 3.93% Keywords: China; intellectual; university

Hangzhou, a city southwest of Shanghai, is freighted with meaning for Shi Yigong. In 1930s, Shi Yigong's grandmother, a Communist, was jailed there by the Nationalist government. She died 18 days after giving birth to his father in prison.

Personal links drew Mr. Shi to Hangzhou when he chose a location for the first private research university in China. He called it Westlake, after the scenic body of water for which the city is famed. The local government's enthusiasm also helped. Hangzhou, though rich and historic, compares unfavourably with Beijing and Shanghai in terms of its intellectual endowment. The local government is keen to host a top-class university.

Mr. Shi's ambitions reach beyond the bounds of the university. His aim is to make China more innovative by adding a dimension to the current educational system. As an

---

4 From The Economist website.

elite university, Westlake will select students on the grounds not just of their test scores, but also of their intellectual maturity and social responsibility. This tends to influence the way pupils are taught at school, and change the way they think. Mr. Shi says: "Westlake is the first such elite university in China. Our future success will result in the establishment of many more."

As the dean of a department at Tsinghua, Mr. Shi has a lot to lose if Westlake does not work. In his favour is the explicit endorsement of the venture by China's president, Xi Jinping. Mr. Xi advocated experiments in higher education. From 2002 to 2007 he was the provincial Party secretary of Zhejiang Province, of which Hangzhou is the capital. During that time Mr. Xi invited an American college, Kean University in New Jersey, to Zhejiang. Its campus is now up and running. Mr. Xi wants China to become an intellectual power as well as an economic one. Against Mr. Shi is the conservatism and rivalrous nature of China's academia. "Everybody is watching him to see if Mr. Shi succeeds or fails," says a colleague. "It's a big risk."

1. **What contributed to Hangzhou's hosting the first private research university in China?**

   A. That Shi Yigong's families used to live in Hangzhou.

   B. That Hangzhou is a historical and prosperous city.

   C. That the local government keenly supported higher education.

   D. That Hangzhou has a great number of top-class universities.

2. **What is Shi Yigong's ambition?**

   A. He aims to make China more innovative through education.

   B. He aims to build the school as an international top university.

   C. Westlake University will select the most intellectual students.

   D. Westlake University will be the best elite university in China.

3. **What can we learn from Paragraph 4?**

   A. President. Xi Jinping supported ventures in higher education.

   B. Mr. Shi has to take challenges to overcome the financial burden.

   C. Kean University was introduced to Hangzhou around 2007.

   D. Mr. Shi's colleagues in Tsinghua are confident in Westlake University's future.

4. What does the underlined word "endorsement" (Line 2, Para. 4) mean?

A. Support.　　B. Objection.　　C. Criticism.　　D. Observation.

5. What is the author's attitude towards Westlake University?

A. Negative.　　B. Positive.　　C. Neutral.　　D. Indifferent.

Reading Skills

Reading for Main Ideas

The main idea of a paragraph is the primary concept that the author is trying to convey to the readers about the topic. It is usually stated clearly in one sentence, but sometimes only suggested by the supporting details. When the main idea of a paragraph is stated, it is most often found in or near the first or last sentence of the paragraph. However, if it is implied, you need to draw an inference from the details.

Stated main idea

Read the passage through to identify the sentence which states the idea generally about the subject under discussion.

Implied main idea

Read the passage thoroughly to find the common connections among all the details and summarize the passage in your own words.

Exercises

Please figure out the main idea of each paragraph.

Paragraph 1

EAP courses can also be in-sessional courses. That is they are taken at the same time as the students' main academic course. In-sessional courses can take one of two forms. They can be seen as language support classes—these are usually free drop-in classes held at lunch-times or Wednesday afternoons and students attend when they are able. Increasingly it is also becoming possible for international students to take credit-bearing EAP courses as part of their degree.

Paragraph 2

Personal links drew Mr. Shi to Hangzhou when he chose a location for the first private research university in China. He called it Westlake, after the scenic body of water for which the city is famed. The local government's enthusiasm also helped. Hangzhou, though rich and historic, compares unfavourably with Beijing and Shanghai in terms of its intellectual endowment. The local government is keen to host a top-class university.

Paragraph 3

If you've decided to go ahead with a double major, then choosing the right courses is an important element for success. See if you can find classes that are related to your two majors so that you can make your credits count for both. You also want to avoid overlap so that you're not working harder than you need to. Finally, use your electives wisely. Often, a major will come with a certain number of elective credits you need to complete, so these can often be put towards your second major. Hence, you should be strategic in your course choices.

THINK

Academic Words in Use

Fill in the blanks in the following sentences with the appropriate words provided in the box below. Change the form of the words if necessary.

academic	lecturer	assess	institution	major	credit
innovative	dimension	maturity	evaluate	document	strategy

1. These problems demonstrate the importance of _____ planning.

2. Oxford and Cambridge Universities are internationally respected _____.

3. The college is noted for its _____ excellence.

4. They couldn't agree on the best way to _____ their students.

5. He is a history _____ at the University of Oklahoma.

6. He is one of the most _____ engineer of his generation.

7. His personality has several _____.

8. Each of these classes is worth three _____.

9. How long does it take for the chicks to grow to _____.

10. Following this critique, students rewrite their papers and submit them for final _____.

11. He was much in demand as a(n) _____ in the US.

12. You should study this _____ with the utmost care.

Writing

For this part, you are allowed 30 minutes to read the following paragraph and continue writing to make it a well-structured article. You should write at least 120 words but no more than 180 words.

Why Do We Attend College?

Attending college can be a prodigious next step for someone freshly graduated from high school. A person with a college diploma gains more opportunities to earn higher income, and leads a more secure and successful life. Higher education meets the social demands for more powerful workplace. Yet college education brings more than career advantages.

Unit 3 Fashion

Viewing

Campus Style: What Does Your Style Mean to You?

About the video clip

This video clip talks about college students' style and what their style means to them.

Understanding the video clip

Match the ideas with the corresponding students according to the video clip.

☐ Sally

A. I think that what you put out into the world is a reflection on your character in a way.

☐ The man with earphones

B. I want more, like from being formal to just comfortable.

☐ The girl with a scarf

C. I think everybody's style is very important in their daily life.

☐ The last interviewee

D. I would call it's really me.

Further thoughts

College life is exciting. You get a chance to re-discover yourself to set on a path for your future and conquer a whole new range of challenges along the way that shapes your personality. Your clothes, for example, have a significant effect on your personality. What is your style and what does your style mean to you? You can refer to the following useful expressions to answer the questions.

Useful expressions
1. I think my current style is... (popular/urban / old school)
2. If you dress well, you'll...
3. shape one's personality
4. affect college students' confidence and personality
5. ...help you grow your social network
6. ...help you perform better
7. improve one's confidence levels / discover new things

Banked Cloze

Below is a passage with ten blanks. You are required to select one word for each blank from the list of choices given in a word bank following the passage. Read the passage carefully before making your choices. Each choice in the bank is identified by a letter. Please write the corresponding letter for each item in the blanks. You may not use any of the words in the bank more than once.

How Do Clothes Affect College Students' Confidence and Personality?[1]

NW: 273 GL: 8 AWL percentage: 3.6% Keywords: dress; confidence; personality

Socializing is among the must-dos while in college, a place you can improve by turning to casual wear. Casual wear makes you 1._____, but remember to keep it within the school's dress 2._____. You don't want to look too revealing as that might give off the wrong idea or too accessorized that it feels forced. Sleek and comfortable casual wear can help you mingle with other students and help you grow your social 3._____. This will improve your confidence levels and let you discover new things.

If you are feeling a little down, then wear colours that uplift your spirit. Bright and

---

1 From itsmyownway website.

cheerful colours can 4._____ improve your moods. As you work through 5._____ times, such as during exams, such a choice could boost your confidence and help you perform better. While working to capture that shape and weight, sporty clothes could be all you need to set a mindset that makes you to keep up with your fitness regimen. 6._____ in a few gym attires, and wear them whether exercising at home or heading out to the gym; they'll improve your endeavours to stay 7._____, not just through exercises but also by making conscious dietary decisions.

Clothes are more than covering your body; if you dress well, you'll feel good, fairly improving your confidence. Considering your dressing as you endeavour to 8._____ and develop your personality might seem insignificant, but it plays a vital role. The best part is that you don't 9._____ have to struggle to keep up with the rapid fashion 10._____; with a few hacks, you can pick a comfortable dressing that works.

A) code	B) challenging	C) greatly
D)trends	E) invest	F) enhance
G) fit	H) amazing	I) network
J) approachable	K) necessarily	L) identify
M) reveal	N) image	O) rule

Long Passage

You are going to read a passage with ten statements attached to it. Each statement contains information given in one of the paragraphs. Identify the paragraph from which the information is derived. You may choose a paragraph more than once. Each paragraph is marked with a letter. Please answer the questions by marking the corresponding letter.

Essential Fashion Tips for College Students[2]

NW: 840 GL: 8.9 AWL percentage: 2.78% Keywords: fashion; clothes; college students

A   Because there is no rule in the book that says a college student can't be fashionable even on a low budget. For the average college student, the goal is not exactly to look amazing but to go to class and survive the rigors of daily studies while navigating life with their roommates or friends. They also might live on their own and has two or three part-time jobs. For this reason, they might not have the time to check out what they wear all the time. Here are some tips to help you improve your fashion sense and the best news is that you don't need tons of money to do so.

B   You might not have much money to work with, or you may have more than enough but durability is an important factor when deciding on the clothes you want to buy. This applies to both ladies' and men's fashion. When you are starting it, always begin with a

---

2 From thefrisky website.

few classic pieces that are guaranteed to last you quite a number of years.

C   When you are a student on a budget, you do not want to spend your money on any clothes you get. You want to instead make sure that everything is great about it before you spend. That means you should never just spend money on clothes that are ill-fitting or bad for the image you want to project, and it is better to actually buy classic pieces.

D   Most fast fashion is poor in quality, but you might not be in a position to buy classic tailored pieces either. However, you can still find a compromise. These are clothes that are durable, look great on you, and are the right quality. In the long term, buying poor quality things is expensive because of replacing them all the time, and it is not worth it.

E   If you want to make great decisions, you will need to be informed. Make sure to do your research, read all the labels, and examine the quality. You will not regret doing this. You are probably familiar with interchangeability. In other words, you are building a wardrobe that has clothes of great quality, all of which can fit very well with each other.

F   For instance, you have two coats, four pairs of pants, and four shirts. If you keep in mind that you can interchange these items, you can come up with 32 possible combinations alone. This makes you realize that you do not need to have an extensive wardrobe full of clothes you might never wear. You simply need a few pieces. Then wear them interchangeably throughout a whole month without wearing them again.

G   Yes, vintage stores. They might seem like they will not offer you much in the way of current fashion. It does not be tempted to resist them. You might just be surprised. The same case goes for flea markets, second-hand shops, thrift shops, vintage fairs, and so on. Many people, unfortunately, make the mistake of thinking that they will become less fashionable if they shop at any of these stores because it seems like they cannot afford great fashion.

H   The truth about all these stores, like the second-hand shops, is they hold infinite chances for your fashion statements. You can get surprisingly great pieces here at an affordable cost; then mix and match them to get amazing outlooks without breaking the bank. You only need to go out to look for it, have the courage to take it, care for it, and mix it with what you already have to give you a sense of pride.

I   This is perhaps the most important advice on here. Whether it is washing them, applying products to extend their lifespan, or brushing these items, it will increase the wears you get from them without having to mend or throw them away.

J   In case they need some extra care, then that is what moms and aunts are for, especially if you have no idea on how to do so. The more you take good care of your clothes, the longer you can use them and that will also mean you do not need to drain the little you already have.

K   In addition, there are fabrics and materials that will need extra care to last as long as possible, like leather. For that reason, you cannot take them to a washing machine, and instead, use the old fashioned way of hand-washing them to guarantee extra care. You will also learn specific products to purchase for specific fabrics, which educates you on the peculiarities of different fabrics and what you can do with them.

L   At the end of the day, you need to take care of what you have, even the clothes you wear. They are an integral part of defining your identity, so you should always aim to keep them in good condition for as long as you can, and still look good even in your college years.

1. You may be very amazed when you visit the vintage stores.

2. When it comes to getting to buy some clothes, durability cannot be neglected.

3. Second-hand stores could be places with reasonable prices that bring you amazing outlooks.

4. Investing in the fast fashion clothes with poor quality is a waste of money in the long run.

5. Clothes need to be taken care of because they are an essential part of who you are.

6. When you wash the clothes you wear, certain products will be much helpful to last their lifespan.

7. If you can make a different combination of your present items of clothes, you will harvest a whole new wardrobe.

8. Students without much money should spend more on classical pieces.

9. Certain fabric and materials should not be taken to the washing machine.

10. You don't need to have a lot of money to improve your fashion sense.

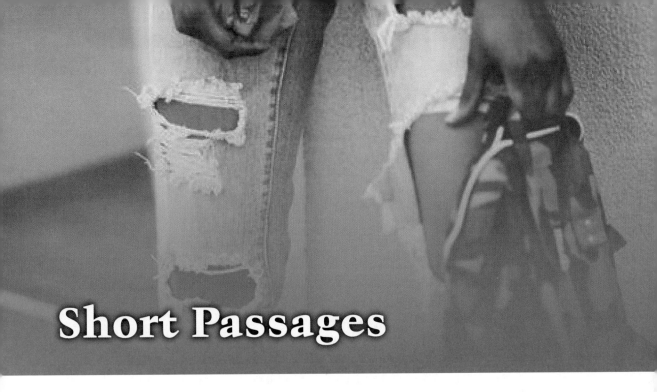

Short Passages

There are 2 passages in this module. Each passage is followed by some questions or unfinished statements. For each of them are four choices marked A, B, C, and D. You should decide on the best choice and mark the corresponding letter.

Passage one

Fashion Trends College Students Are Obsessed with[3]

NW: 381   GL: 8   AWL percentage: 3.31%   Keywords: clothes; outfit; style

College campus is a place where you have a great possibility to show off your fashionable clothes and great speeches, send a message of self-confidence, determination, and trust. During your education at college, it is very important to find your personal style because that will help you become a more confident person.

Here are a few fashion trends that make any college student get obsessed with.

Cute T-shirts with a college color, name or logo on the front are very popular. Your wardrobe can't be complete without an item of clothing that shows off your college spirit. They give interest to any pair of jeans or shorts. Reserve several for the dorm but do not

---

3   From qrius website.

forget about a couple of must-have for lessons and special occasions.

The jeans are easy and comfortable to wear. All students wear them every day and anywhere, in class, to have fun in the college dorm, <u>entertain</u> at a free college event or just go for a walk. They can be styled with everything like sneakers, heels and basic tees. Most of the graduates keep at least 4 pairs of jeans in their wardrobe. The denim trousers can be of any style from dark-washed skinnies to light blue high-waisted jeans. You can choose any cut and color that you feel most comfortable in.

It doesn't matter what brand you prefer, bright sneakers of different colors—white, green, orange, purple or a combination of several colors—are a real hit this season. They show style, comfort, and youth. They are practical, comfy and on trend. They are also perfect for walking to college lectures or dancing in a club. Add a "wow" factor to your style with a new pair of colorful sneakers.

To sum it up, the best outfit you can wear is that when you break the rules. Wear the clothes that make you feel confident and full of self-love. Remember the rule: we learn the character of a person through experience and interaction; a person's appearance is what appeals us at first sight. With all these tips, you can easily update your wardrobes to be more fashionable forward.

1. **How will finding your personal style help you?**

A. It drives you to demonstrate yourself more often.

B. It turns you into a person of greater confidence.

C. It makes you more sensitive to fashion trends.

D. It allows others to trust you more.

2. **What can make your wardrobe complete?**

A. Sunglasses.

B. Jeans.

C. Sneakers.

D. T-shirts.

3. **What can go with everything like sneakers, heels and basic tees?**

A. T-shirts.

B. Jeans.

C. Sneakers.

D. Belts.

4. What does the underlined word "entertain" (Line 2, Para. 4) mean?

   A. Amuse.

   B. Appear.

   C. Occur.

   D. Wander.

5. What suggestion is given about the clothes that you should wear?

   A. The clothes that can show your shape.

   B. The clothes that are quite popular.

   C. The clothes that make you feel confident.

   D. The clothes that the fashion icons like.

Passage two

Do Clothes Make the Student?[4]

NW: 430 GL: 6.9 AWL percentage: 2.16% Keywords: student; dress; comfort

I've been teaching college for many years, long enough to note the steady relaxation of attention in matters of student dress. I've long grown used to the torn jeans, flip-flops, shorts in the dead of the Maine winter, and ball caps worn backward. Still, I took note recently when one of my students showed up in pajama bottoms. I couldn't help remarking, "Did you just roll out of bed?"

His response: "Five minutes ago."

I grew up in a working-class family. My parents were World War II and Depression vintage and they came of age under conditions of poverty. Perhaps this is why "looking sharp", as my father used to put it, was so important.

I smile when I think back on the occasions that my parents associated with needing to look presentable. Once, when I was 14 and my brother 12, my father announced that he was taking us into Manhattan (just a subway ride away) to see the debut of "2001: A Space Odyssey." My brother and I were giddy at the prospect, but were momentarily deflated

---

4 From csmonitor website.

when my father directed us to put on our best clothes, including jackets and ties. "But why?" I begged, not wanting to change out of my comfortable jeans, T-shirt, and sneakers.

"Because," he said, "we're going to New York."

I can still see the stars in his eyes as he uttered these words.

So yes, I'm all for freedom of choice in matters of dress, and yes, I do want my students to be comfortable. But I also want to pay my respects to those students who believe that appearances count.

I think of the woman, a somewhat older, so-called nontraditional student I had in class a few years back. She was someone to whom science did not come easily: She worked doggedly for respectable grades on every assignment. But I was struck by how tastefully she dressed, day after day.

When the course ended, I took a moment to mention this to her. "You always looked so nice," I remarked. "As if you were ready to take on the world."

Without missing a beat, she answered, as if it were self-evident, "I've waited 12 years to return to school, and I dress up to remind myself to be serious about it."

And, I might add, she seemed perfectly comfortable to me.

1. **What has the author long grown used to in matters of student dress?**

A. The suits of boys.

B. The pajamas of girls.

C. The torn jeans and shorts.

D. The sunglasses in the matter of student dress.

2. **What can we learn about the author's parents from Paragraph 3?**

A. They were keen on fashionable items.

B. They valued the importance of looking decent.

C. They related their dressing code to their status.

D. They cared little about what to wear.

3. **What does the underlined word "presentable" (Line 2, Para. 4) mean?**

A. Capable.

B. Suitable.

C. Affordable.

D. Available.

4. **What is the author's attitude towards the students' choice in dressing?**

A. He really cares about the style of the students.

B. He has a problem with the torn jeans of the students.

C. He aims to improve the fashion taste of the students.

D. He respects the students' freedom of choice.

5. **What is the author's purpose of writing about the student he had in class a few years back?**

A. To remind the readers of the importance of comfort dressing.

B. To compliment the woman's way of dressing.

C. To devalue the woman's taste of dressing.

D. To emphasize the importance of dressing nicely.

Reading Skills

Finding out Thesis Statement

Articles and essays are both composed of individual paragraphs linked together in the same way a chain is linked together to produce a sustained piece of writing that may be a single page to 20 or more pages. Whatever the length, the writer of an article has in mind a focus or a point, which, like the main idea of a paragraph, may be stated or implied. This main idea is called the thesis or thesis statement. A thesis statement directly answers the question asked of you. A thesis is an interpretation of a question or subject, not the question or subject itself. The subject, or topic, of an essay might be World War II or *Moby Dick*; a thesis must then offer a way to understand the war or the novel. A writer may place the thesis near the beginning of the essay, in the middle, or at the end, but usually it comes somewhere near the beginning. In addition, a thesis might be two sentences, though rarely more than that.

Exercises

Please read the above reading skill of finding out thesis statement and use the skill to locate the thesis statement of the two passages in this unit.

Passage 1: Fashion Trends College Students Are Obsessed with

Passage 2: Do Clothes Make the Student?

THINK

Academic Words in Use

Fill in the blanks in the following sentences with the appropriate words in their proper forms. Change the form of the words if necessary.

identify	survive	invest	somewhat	trend	freedom
relax	interact	tradition	significant	fairly	approach

1. Our boss dislikes being overburdened with _____ detail.

2. There is a growing _____ towards earlier retirement.

3. Despite being a big star, she's very _____.

4. He _____ his life savings in his daughter's business.

5. Scientists have _____ a link between diet and cancer.

6. He needs that amount of money to _____.

7. _____ teaching methods sometimes only succeed in putting students off learning.

8. His theories are _____ remote from reality.

9. As soon as I had made the final decision, I felt a lot more_____ .

10. As a big company, it's important to build a good _____ with staff.

11. We must never undervalue _____ and equality.

12. You've got to be _____ single-minded about it.

Writing

For this part, you are allowed 30 minutes to read the following paragraphs and continue writing to make a well-structured article. You should write at least 120 words but no more than 180 words.

Good and Bad Effects of Fashion on Students

Today's youths are totally influenced by new fashion trends. They tend to follow fashion styles in order to look different and stylish in front of others by wearing different types of clothes and accessories.

As we can see, there are good and bad effects of fashion on students. _____

_____

_____

_____

_____

_____

_____

Unit 4 Food Is Culture

Viewing

What Breakfast Looks like Around the World

About the video clip

    While enjoying your favourite breakfast dish, have you ever wondered what people from other countries eat to start the day? This video clip introduces some iconic breakfast dishes around the world.

Understanding the video clip

Matching

    What are the dishes like? Below are some of the dishes that are mentioned in the video clip. Match the pictures with the corresponding statements.

1. _____   2. _____   3. _____

4. _____   5. _____

A. It is preferred by people from England.

B. It is enjoyed by people from Japan.

C. It is liked by American people.

D. This dish is thought to be originated from Tunisia.

E. It often consists of miso soup, fish and steamed rice.

F. This dish is sometimes referred to as a "fry-up".

G. It is a flaky pastry that can be eaten hot and cold.

H. The dish features a fried egg, sausage, fried bread, bacon, beans and tomatoes, paired with a side of hot tea.

Fill in the blanks

Now watch the video clip again and fill in the blanks in the table below.

Country or region	Iconic breakfast dish	Characteristics
Morocco	Sfenj	Breakfast in Morocco is all about _____.
The Mediterranean Region	Shakshuka	The dish features eggs _____, _____ or scrambled in a savoury tomato-based sauce.
England	Full English breakfast	Having this dish means _____.
Japan	Traditional Japanese breakfast	It includes an array of savoury bites.
Philippines	Tapsilog	A Pilipino breakfast starts with _____, _____ and savoury flavours.
The United States	Eggs, bacon, toast and pancakes	Breakfast in the US tends to include a few regular go-tos.
India and Pakistan	Halwa Poori	Deep fried Poori served with curry and Halwa.
Myanmar	Mohinga Soup	This dish is a _____ and _____ with lemongrass, garlic and catfish.
Turkey	Kahvalti	Breakfast in Turkey consists of _____, black and green olives, fresh baked _____, fruit preserves, _____, sweet butter and black tea.
Columbia	Changua	A hearty soup dish made of _____, water, scallions and eggs.
Bulgaria	Banitsa	The dish is a traditional pastry.
Maldives	Mas huni	It is a traditional breakfast dish that uses ____, chilies, onions and _____ as ingredients.

Further thoughts

People from different countries have different preferences for breakfast. What about Chinese breakfast dishes and your favourite ones? Please list some Chinese breakfast dishes and introduce their characteristics.

Chinese breakfast dish	Characteristics
Pancakes (*Jianbing*)	It is an iconic Chinese breakfast from northern China and is arguably the "king of breakfast" in China. *Jianbing* is commonly wrapped around a deep-fried thin dough, and topped with ingredients like eggs, scallions, coriander and a savoury sauce.
Dim sum	Dim sum is extremely popular in southern China, especially in Guangdong Province. Dim sum includes a wide range of dishes like shrimp dumplings, spring rolls and porridge.
…	…

Banked Cloze

Below is a passage with ten blanks. You are required to select one word for each blank from the list of choices given in a word bank following the passage. Read the passage carefully before making your choices. Each choice in the blank is identified by a letter. Please write the corresponding letter for each item in the blanks. You may not use any of the words in the bank more than once.

In China, Cheese Is Strange, but Pizza Is Hot[1]

NW: 265 GL: 8.4 **AWL percentage:** 2.26% **Keywords:** cheese; pizza; China

China may be the hardest place in the world to sell cheese, but Liu Yang has been trying anyway—and Western fast food may be his salvation.

There has not been diary in the mainstream Chinese diet for centuries—no 1. _____, no milk, no cheese, nothing. So when Mr. Liu opened a two-room cheese shop on the outskirts of Beijing five years ago, "People said, 'What is this strange stinky thing?'" He 2. _____. "'How am I supposed to eat it?'" Mr. Liu's offerings of cheeses at first mystified Chinese customers, even though 3. _____ was driving demand for other European luxuries. He 4. _____ sells about 33 pounds of cheese a day, and he hopes to do better as more Chinese become 5. _____ with the stuff.

---

1 From *The New York Times* by Hernandez J.

That is already happening, albeit through a side door: a(n) 6._____ appetite for American-style fast food. The 7. _____ Chinese city dweller eats it at least once a week, by one estimate; Pizza Hut is opening stores in China at a rate of about one a day. Pizza, of course, 8. _____ cheese. Theo Spierings, chief executive of Fonterra, a New Zealand dairy producer, said pizza's popularity was driving up demand for cheese across Asia. Supermarkets in big cities are starting to put blocks of cheese on 9._____. And China's imports of cheese rose 70 percent from 2009 to 2014, according to Mintel, a market research company.

Cheese was regarded to be too barbaric for the national diet. That stigma is gone, but for many shoppers, another one 10. _____. "I'm afraid it will make me fat," said Zhao Lin, 32, of Beijing.

A) recalled	B) average	C) contains
D) popularity	E) merely	F) butter
G) growing	H) ordinary	I) currently
J) certainly	K) remains	L) acquainted
M) display	N) prosperity	O) expected

Long Passage

You are going to read a passage with ten statements attached to it. Each statement contains information given in one of the paragraphs. Identify the paragraph from which the information is derived. You may choose a paragraph more than once. Each paragraph is marked with a letter. Please answer the questions by writing the corresponding letter after the statements.

Food and Culture[2]

NW: 992 GL: 9 AWL percentage: 4.17% Keywords: food; diet; culture

A   People from different cultural backgrounds eat different foods. The ingredients, ways of preparation, and types of food eaten at different meals vary among cultures. The places in which families live—and where their ancestors originated—influence food likes and dislikes. These food preferences result in patterns of food choices within a cultural or regional group.

B   Food items themselves have meaning attached to them. In many Western countries, a box of chocolates would be viewed as a suitable gift. The recipient of the gift would react differently to a gift of cabbage or carrots than to chocolate. In other countries, chocolates might be considered a less suitable gift.

2 From JRank website.

C   Nations or countries are frequently associated with certain foods. For example, many people associate Italy with pizza and pasta. Yet Italians eat many other foods, and types of pasta dishes are different throughout Italy. Ways of preparation and types of food also vary by regions of a nation. Some families in the United States prefer to eat "meat and potatoes", but "meat and potatoes" are not eaten on a regular basis, nor even preferred, by many in the United States. And it would not be regarded as a national cuisine. Grits, a coarsely ground corn that is boiled, is eaten in the southern United States. A package of grits can only be found in the largest supermarkets in the upper Midwest and is difficult to find even in large Midwestern supermarkets.

D   Regional food habits do exist, but they also change over time. As people move from one country to another, food practices and preferences are imported and exported. Families move to other places, bringing their food preferences with them. They may use their old recipes with new ingredients, or experiment with new recipes, incorporating ingredients to match their own tastes. In addition, food itself is imported from other countries. Around 80% of Samoa's food requirements are imported from the United States, New Zealand, or Australia. Because people and food are mobile, attempts to characterize a country or people by what they eat are often inaccurate.

E   Nevertheless, what is considered edible in some parts of the world might be considered inedible in other parts. The values or beliefs a society gives to cooking ingredients characterize what families within a cultural group will eat. For example, both plant and animal sources may help people to meet nutritional requirements for protein; soybeans, beef, pork are all important protein sources. Yet, due to the symbolism attached to these protein sources, they are not equally preferred by all societies.

F   Some food beliefs and practices are due to religious beliefs. Around the world, Muslims fast during Ramadan[3]. During this month, Muslims fast during daylight hours, eating and drinking before dawn and after sunset. Orthodox Jews and some conservative Jews follow dietary laws, the kosher diet[4]. The dietary laws, which describe the use and preparation of animal foods, are followed for purposes of spiritual health. Many followers of Buddhism, Hinduism, and Jainism[5] are vegetarians, in part, because of a doctrine of noninjury or nonviolence. Abstinence from eating meat in these traditions stems from the desire to avoid harming other living creatures.

G   In addition to impacting food choices, culture also influences food-related

---

3   Ramadan: 莱麦丹月, 穆斯林的斋月, 是十二个月份中最神圣的月份

4   kosher diet: 符合犹太教饮食规定的食材

5   Buddhism, Hinduism, and Jainism: 佛教、印度教和耆那教

etiquette. People in Western societies may refer to food-related etiquette as table manners, a phrase that demonstrates the cultural expectation of eating food or meals at a table. Some people eat with forks and spoons; more people use fingers or chopsticks. However, utensil choice is much more complicated than choosing chopsticks, fingers, or flatware. Among some groups who primarily eat food with their fingers, diners use only the right hand to eat. Some people use only three fingers of the right hand. Among other groups, use of both hands is acceptable. In some countries, licking the fingers is polite; in others, licking the fingers is considered impolite. Rules regarding polite eating may

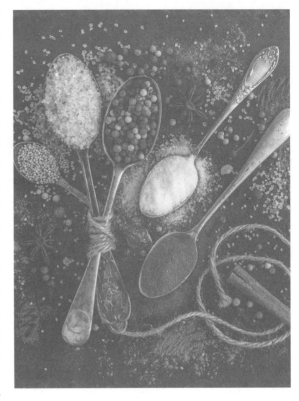

increase in formal settings. At some formal dinners, a person might be expected to choose the "right" fork to match the food being eaten at a certain point in the meal.

H   The amount people eat and leave uneaten also differs from group to group. Some people from Middle Eastern and Southeast Asian countries might leave a little bit of food on their plates. This means that their hunger has been satisfied. However, cooks from other countries might be offended if food is left on the plate, indicating that the guest may have disliked the food. Likewise, a clean plate might mean either satisfaction with the meal or desire for more food.

I   Even the role of conversation during mealtime is different from place to place. Many families believe that mealtime is a good time to chat and to "catch up" on the lives of family and friends. Among other families, conversation during a meal is acceptable, but the topics of conversation are limited. In some Southeast Asian countries, it is considered polite to limit conversation during a meal.

J   Food plays an important role in the lives of families in most cultures. However, the degree of importance varies from one culture to another. For example, in American Samoa most family activities and ceremonies centre on eating. A host family shows its prosperity or societal rank by providing large quantities of food. Among other families in other places, activities and celebrations include food, but food is not necessarily the centre of the event.

K   Food traditions differ greatly throughout the world. Even among people who share similar backgrounds and some of the same food habits, eating patterns are not exactly the same. Further, families vary from their own daily routines on holidays, when travelling, or when guests are present. Men eat differently from women. People of different age groups eat differently. However, in most parts of the world, food is associated with hospitality and expression of friendship. Therefore, sensitivity to food rules and customs is important in building and strengthening cross-cultural relationships.

1. People's eating patterns differ even within a cultural group. ☐

2. People's preference for food might change as they immigrate. ☐

3. The religions that people believe in affect people's food choices. ☐

4. Rules related to eating are very complicated and they vary from culture to culture. ☐

5. Families from certain cultures enjoy chatting when having meals. ☐

6. Food items mean differently to people from different countries. ☐

7. The degree of importance that people give to food varies across cultures. ☐

8. People have fixed ideas about what other people eat in a certain country. ☐

9. The values people give to certain food items influence their preference. ☐

10. The amount of food left uneaten means differently in different cultures. ☐

Short Passages

There are 2 passages in this module. Each passage is followed by some questions or unfinished statements. For each of them are four choices marked A, B, C, and D. You should decide on the best choice and mark the corresponding letter.

Passage one

How to Order Dim Sum?[6]

NW: 358 GL: 7.8 AWL percentage: 5.48% Keywords: dim sum; dumplings; shrimp

Whether you're a newcomer to dim sum or an <u>avid</u> enthusiast, Sandy Shi, executive dim sum chef at the Wynn Las Vegas hotel, has tips on how to find the best dim sum restaurants, and what to order when you get there.

Dim sum is traditionally meant to be experienced with a group. As a native Hongkonger, Shi sees the cuisine as a communal activity rather than just a meal. To her, "dim sum is an event for friends and family" where they gather in large numbers to leisurely enjoy simple dishes together. Aside from the cultural significance, there's a practical reason to eat dim sum with a large group: you get to try as many of the

---

6 From *Time* by Kang A.

shareable bites as possible.

A newcomer to dim sum should try the essentials: *har gow*[7] or shrimp dumplings; *siu mai*[8], another style of dumpling typically made with pork and shrimp; and guo tie, or potstickers. These are fundamentals in a dim sum chef's repertoire, Shi says, and you should avoid restaurants that mess up the basics. A more advanced dim sum dish Shi suggests is fried shrimp balls. They are "particularly hard to make because they are crispy on the outside and have a hot broth on the inside". If the restaurant nails this menu item, that means it has a skilled chef in the kitchen.

Drinking tea is an important part of the dim sum experience that you shouldn't skip, says Shi. In fact, because the beverage has had a longstanding association with the cuisine, yum cha, which literally means "drink tea" in Cantonese, is used interchangeably with the phrase "dim sum".

A truly great dim sum place will use fresh seafood. In Shi's kitchen, she and her team make *har gow* with fresh, whole shrimp; lesser restaurants might try to hide that their shrimp is not fresh by mashing it up for the dumpling filling. Additionally, lower-quality dim sum spots may not freshly wrap their dumplings, and then overcook them to hide that fact. One way to tell if a place is cutting corners is that its dumplings will break apart when you pick them up.

1. **What does the underlined word "avid" (Line 1, Para. 1) mean?**

A. Hungry.

B. Keen.

C. Patient.

D. Indifferent.

2. **What does a native Hongkonger generally think of dim sum?**

A. Having dim sum alone is fancy and economical.

B. Eating dim sum is a chance for family members to gather together.

C. Sharing dim sum with others means you will not get the dim sum you want.

D. Eating dim sum with many people is not a good way to enjoy dim sum.

---

7 *har gow*: 虾饺

8 *siu mai*: 烧卖

3. **Why does Sandy Shi suggest a newcomer to dim sum to try the essentials?**

   A. Because the classics represent the skillfulness of a dim sum chef.

   B. Because the classics are hard for a dim sum chef to make.

   C. Because the classics are freshly made by dim sum chefs.

   D. Because the classics are the threshold for a qualified restaurant.

4. **How do lower-quality restaurants make dim sums?**

   A. Use whole shrimp as filling.

   B. Wrap dumplings freshly.

   C. Use ready-made dumplings.

   D. Overcook dumplings that use fresh fillings.

5. **What would be a suggested way to enjoy dim sum according to the passage?**

   A. Eat the classics and drink tea on one's own.

   B. Have *siu mai* and potstickers with no beverage.

   C. Share the newly invented dish with family members.

   D. Enjoy freshly made *har gow* and tea with a group of friends.

Passage two

The Battle for Breakfast[9]

NW: 367 GL: 8.6 AWL percentage: 2.12% Keywords: breakfast; China; chain

Like everyone else, Chinese people love fast food. Western salty, fatty fast-food chains such as McDonald's and KFC serve up vast quantities of lunch and dinner to the world's most populous nation. But not breakfast. Chinese consumers have yet to be won over by the Egg McMuffin or even the breakfast platter. No Western fast-food chain has figured out how to please hungry Chinese mouths in the morning.

---

9 From The Economist website.

Paul French of Mintel, a research firm, reckons that the Chinese foreign fast-food market, valued at RMB 87.8 ($13.9) billion, is "underpenetrated" at breakfast time. Only 21% of Chinese eat fast food in the morning, compared to over 75% at lunch time. Why is this? "People want congee for breakfast, not a sausage sandwich," says Mr. French.

Domestic restaurants see a gap in the market, and are rising early to fill it. They are copying the foreigners' chief selling points—fashionable decor and clean tables—but keeping the menu strictly Chinese. Local fast-food chains such as Manfadu and 82 degrees are building new stores with plastic menus and western-style layouts. They serve congee with pickled vegetables and youtiao (deep-fried dough). Hungry locals flock in. Mr. French reckons that 82 degrees is opening two stores a week to meet growing demand. He also reckons Manfadu now holds 10% of the Shanghai breakfast market, up from 2% in 2008.

McDonald's, which has got away with selling the same breakfast products everywhere with a few minor tweaks (an Egg McMuffin with chicken is an option in China), may have to think harder. Though breakfast accounts for around a quarter of the firm's American sales, in China this number is less than 10%. McDonald's says it is playing the long game. "We know breakfast isn't going to be an overnight sensation," says Jessica Lee, a senior director in McDonald's Asia, "it wasn't in the US either."

McDonald's are making inroads into the breakfast market with new combinations, "the egg McMuffin with chicken is selling well," says Miss Lee. But the company's commitment to their current model of minor tweaking rather than truly new products may hold them back. They should heed the Chinese proverb, "do not fear going forward slowly, fear standing still."

1. **What does the underlined word "chains" (Line 1, Para. 1) mean?**

A. Dishes.

B. Delicacies.

C. Companies.

D. Stores.

2. **What can we learn from Paragraph 2?**

A. The value of Chinese foreign fast-food market is small.

B. Chinese people prefer sandwiches to congee for breakfast.

C. Foreign companies have earned a lot from the Chinese breakfast market.

D. Chinese foreign fast-food market is still underdeveloped at breakfast time.

3. **What are Chinese fast-food chains doing to fill the gap in the Chinese breakfast market?**

A. Adding Western breakfast dishes to their menu.

B. Opening new stores and publishing advertisements.

C. Localizing the breakfast products sold by foreign brands.

D. Serving Chinese breakfast dishes on clean tables and in fashionable stores.

4. **What is the author's attitude towards McDonald's breakfast plan in China?**

A. Disapproving.

B. Indifferent.

C. Positive.

D. Ambiguous.

5. **What can we infer from the passage?**

A. Most Chinese people do not like Western fastfood.

B. Chinese companies can compete with Western fastfood chains in the breakfast market.

C. McDonald's has introduced truly new breakfast dishes for Chinese customers.

D. McDonald's is not good at selling breakfast either in China or abroad.

Reading Skills

Recognizing Essential Sentence Elements

All sentences, even the most complex ones, are built from some basic elements: subjects, verbs, objects and complements. The most important of these are subjects and verbs: a sentence is incomplete without someone (subjects) performing the action (verbs). When reading a passage, especially when doing extensive reading, it is a useful skill to first locate the subject and verb of a sentence. In this way, you can quickly grasp the main idea of a complex sentence and gradually increase your reading speed as you practise. To recognize the subjects and verbs, consider the following suggestions:

1. Find the verb first

Always locate the verb first when you try to understand the main idea of a sentence. Once you have recognized the verb, ask yourself, "Who or what is doing the action or being described?" and the answer to the question is the subject of the sentence.

e.g.: People from different cultural backgrounds eat different foods.

"Eat" is the verb. Who or what eats? "Cultural backgrounds" can't eat, so "people" is the subject of this sentence.

2. Understand the structure of the verb

Different from Chinese, a verb in English might consist of one or more than one word.

Some auxiliary verbs might be added before the main verb to indicate the tense, voice, mood and other grammatical meaning of the action. Phrasal verbs, which consist of a verb and one or more than one particle, are also extremely common in English sentences.

e.g.: Cheese was regarded to be too barbaric for the national diet.

In this sentence, "was regarded" is the verb. The two-word verb suggests that the action is passive and happens in the past.

3. Distinguish the infinitive and the main verb

If a verb follows the infinitive marker "to", then it is not the main verb of the sentence. The main verb that you should look for is either before or after the infinitive.

e.g.: Lesser restaurants might try to hide that their shrimp is not fresh.

"To hide" is the infinitive and the main verb of this sentence is "try".

4. Understand word orders in English

Similar to Chinese, the most common and basic sentence pattern in English is Subject-Verb-Object (SVO). No matter how long or how complex a sentence is, the word order rarely changes. Having an understanding of the standard word order of English sentences might help you to distinguish subjects and verbs.

Exercises

Please read the following sentences quickly and underline the subjects with a solid line and the verbs with a wavy line.

1. The amount people eat and leave uneaten also differs from group to group. Some people from Middle Eastern and Southeast Asian countries might leave a little bit of food on their plates.

2. Like everyone else, Chinese people love fast food. Western salty, fatty fast-food chains such as McDonald's and KFC serve up vast quantities of lunch and dinner to the world's most populous nation.

3. Nevertheless, what is considered edible in some parts of the world might be considered inedible in other parts. The values or beliefs a society gives to cooking ingredients characterize what families within a cultural group will eat.

THINK

Academic Words in Use

Fill in the blanks in the following sentences with the appropriate words provided in the box below. Change the form of the words if necessary.

vary	classic	react	feature	regional	source
percent	domestic	minor	immigrant	demonstrate	inaccurate

1. It is often stated that we use only 10 _____ of our brain.

2. Blue and white is the _____ color combination for bathrooms.

3. I wonder how he would _____ if he tastes this delicious dish.

4. The quality of the students' work _____ considerably.

5. He is a(n) _____ from Africa and he enjoys life in China.

6. By next year, the revenue of _____ and global brands will be equal.

7. At the meeting, he _____ his designs to his customers with a PowerPoint.

8. A key _____ of Chinese cuisine is stir-frying ingredients with a wok.

9. Reviewing requires _____ efforts but offers major benefits.

10. It is widely recognized that there are 8 _____ cuisines in China.

11. The report is badly researched and quite _____.

12. Tourism is a major _____ of income for this area.

Writing

For this part, you are allowed 30 minutes to write a short passage to briefly introduce your favourite Chinese food. You should write at least 120 words but no more than 180 words.

My Favorite Chinese Food

Unit 5 East or West, Home Is Best

Viewing

About the video clip

    This video clip discusses the meanings of home. People give their understandings of "home".

Understanding the video clip

    With the development of technologies and economies, people have a much better life ever than before. So more and more people leave their old homes and move into skyscrapers. Watch the video clip and listen carefully. Find out what home means to them and fill in the blanks.

1. People say they _____ in the valley _____ it's a bad thing.

2. Home just means: _____ , cars, girls, _____ , family.

3. It doesn't matter _____ . You've got everything _____ right here.

4. If you look for them, there are _____ in this universe than you _____ .

5. Honestly, _____ I go, this always be home with me.

6. Home _____ you, take it with you and you'll always be home.

Further thoughts

In the following table, there are some proverbs about home. Try to understand those proverbs and write down the translations of those proverbs in the second column and put down your understandings in the third column.

Proverbs about home	Translations of the proverbs	Your understandings towards the proverbs
1. East or west, home is best.		
2. Although the sun shines, leave not your cloak at home.		
3. Charity begins at home, but should not end there.		
4. A book holds a house of gold.		
5. Home is home, though never so homely.		
6. Home is where the heart is.		

Banked Cloze

Below is a passage with ten blanks. You are required to select one word for each blank from the list of choices given in a word bank following the passage. Read the passage carefully before making your choices. Each choice in the blank is identified by a letter. Please write the corresponding letter for each item in the blanks. You may not use any of the words in the bank more than once.

There Is No Place like Home[1]

NW: 282 GL: 7.8 AWL percentage: 2.25% Keywords: live; home; person

Every person has a place which he or she treats differently from any other. It is the place where he feels more 1. _____ than anywhere else. It is not exactly the place where the person lives. Sometimes, it may be some house or flat from the past, for example, the one he or she lived in during childhood. But what is so 2. _____ about it that it plays such an important role in the culture of many nations of the world?

I think it is because a person's home 3. _____ as the best reflection of a personality on the 4. _____ world. It is true even if someone doesn't spend most of his/her time at home; at least they spend it there 5. _____. It could even be more true when one can say a lot about a person judging by his clothes.

---

1 From Paperwritings website.

One cannot live somewhere for years without leaving a kind of trail. You can judge about the 6. _____ of people by simply looking at the way they decorate or the place where they are living. I want to mention here the 7. _____ of the way things are arranged. It doesn't matter whether the place is kept in apple-pie order or not. It is clearly understood that a person 8. _____ influences the place of living, because even if a house is fully furnished but uninhabited, one will immediately feel it upon entering. Eventually, the 9. _____ a man lives somewhere, the more his home reminds of him when he looks at it. It probably won't give you too much useful information, but still may be helpful in terms of 10. _____ impression.

A) undoubtedly	B) regards	C) specific
D) outside	E) longer	F) shorter
G) overall	H) comfortable	I) effect
J) affect	K) regularly	L) probably
M) majority	N) species	O) serves

Long Passage

You are going to read a passage with ten statements attached to it. Each statement contains information given in one of the paragraphs. Identify the paragraph from which the information is derived. You may choose a paragraph more than once. Each paragraph is marked with a letter. Please answer the questions by writing the corresponding letter after the statements.

Home, Sweet Home[2]

NW: 1,091 GL: 8.6 AWL percentage: 3.94% Keywords: memories; homesick; meaning

A   Each one of us has the place, which brings back good memories. It is the symbol of comfort and wellness. It evokes memories related to music, objects, colors, people, and dishes. This place is called home. It is kept in our memories as an ideal one, even if it is not so perfect. Home serves as a kind of fortress to freedom, our deeds and us.

B   The word "home" is a many-faceted word that combines different ideas. Home is culture, religion, the place where you live, friends, relatives, neighbors, cuisine, personal objects and environment. Home should be the place where you feel safe, free and in the state of health and physical well-being. It is often associated with parents, siblings, warmth and comfort. However, international students do suffer a lot from this psychological

---

2 From Grades Fixer website.

sickness. When they lose at least one of these, they feel homesick and start to understand the meaning of the word "home".

C   Home is considered as a place where you were brought up. It is related to the childhood, toys, favorite dishes, and traditions. Sometimes it happens for those international students while in the middle of the school day when they have a very strong desire to go home. They close their eyes and see unforgettable masterpieces—a kitchen, a cozy bedroom, a living room, a bathroom, or soft carpet under the feet. It is related to their best memories, family, relatives and history. Generally, these images are the houses of our grandparents or parents. In these places the family gathers and has a wonderful time together. They bring back warm memories about the childhood and family holidays. Even music and flavors may make them think about their home. Any person may miss home when he is away for educational reasons.

D   In fact, close relations to home cause the feeling of homesickness. In order to find an academic chance abroad, international students leave their homes, families, and friends. Being in a different country, they feel very sad about the places, objects, people, buildings and culture. In spite of modern technologies, this feeling is still very common for international students. It may affect the person's behavior and mental well-being. Those students often miss every single object at their home. And that is why home is a varied and rich union of family and personal objects.

E   Some people evaluate objects found at home. A guest cannot notice special elements of design in one's home. It can be a piece of furniture or decoration developed or made by one of the family members. Or it can be pictures or valuable things which are passed from generation to generation. People show very strong connections and relations to personal mementos.

F   Even rooms, whether it is a kitchen or living room, is one of the mementos which bring their memories back. In this way, home may express different aspects of our past. It is the place directly connected with our biography, as here we had physical and special representation. In addition, it is the place where we live, keep our properties, have a rest, receive guests, spend leisure, eat, drink, and watch TV etc. You come home after a hard day, take a bath, lie on the sofa and do anything you want. You have freedom of actions.

G   Such a house or an apartment may have a link to your past at the same time being a door to the future. In such a house you feel comfortable; you come back to the house willingly and with great desire. For someone it may be a huge cottage, or a house at the seaside, for others a tiny one room flat with a kitchen. The size of your home does not mean anything. The things inside it mean all. It should have something to do with physical state in which we feel mentally relaxed.

H The memories become related to the house itself, a building where we grew up. When we think about our country as a home, the feeling of homesick begins. In this case, there are several reasons of being homesick and culture shock is one of them. International students, especially those who do not understand the language well, and who come from countries with different cultural backgrounds, have troubles getting used to the surrounding environment. The greater the differences between the host culture and the native culture, the stronger feeling of homesickness will the students experience.

I Reasons are various. Culture shock causes desire for family and familiar surroundings. The second reason is time difference, which sometimes makes communication with relatives almost impossible. They start feeling lonely except the cases when they can make friends easily. Language is considered to be the third reason of homesickness. Sometimes international students do not speak perfectly, do not understand the professor, and cannot express their ideas. These factors may cause a great trouble for any international student.

J As a result, the effects include sadness, loneliness, sleeping problems, headaches, anxiety, isolation, and difficulties at the university or college. Unfortunately the feeling of homesickness is long lasting and may lead to social alienation. According to some studies, students who study far away from their houses experience the feeling of homesickness more often than those who study close to their parents. Those who feel homesick often have poor progress in studying, get lower scores, and are more often depressed in comparison to students who are not homesick.

K Home is a word, which embraces and has very vast meaning. It reflects our values and beliefs that are usually associated with the childhood deep in our memories. If anything reminds us about any aspect of beliefs or values, there will be no doubt that you will immediately think about home. In this context, home is defined by neighborhood and ethnic group.

L Home is a place of memories, with certain design, traditions and technology. It is also a place for practical and social activities. In many cases people start appreciating home after moving out, changing the place of living or losing relatives. Only after it the person begins to realize how deep the meaning of the word is, how important it is to keep relation to our home.

M In this case the proverb "East or west, home is best" is really true. A home holds our family and cultural heritage, history of whole generations, reflects acceptance and limitless warmth. Being a form of love, it is associated with a tree, which has deep roots. You feel at home, you feel comfortable and at ease in the place you are.

1. Unforgettable masterpieces at home may make the international students think about their home. ☐

2. People cherish the items at home, and they show strong connections to them. ☐

3. Home symbolizes comfort and wellness and it is a kind of fortress to freedom. ☐

4. The word "home" combines various meanings and is concerned with different people and different kinds of feelings. ☐

5. Only after experiencing the change of lives can people truly realize the deep meaning of home. ☐

6. Homesickness will result in some negative effects for university or college students. ☐

7. Culture shock, time difference and language are the key reasons of being homesick. ☐

8. Home is a form of love, which is like a tree with deep roots. ☐

9. In spite of modern technologies, the feeling of homesickness is still common for the international students. ☐

10. It is not the outside of a home or the size of a home, but the things inside of the home that mean all. ☐

Short Passages

There are 2 passages in this module. Each passage is followed by some questions or unfinished statements. For each passage there are four choices marked A, B, C, and D. You should decide on the best choice and mark the corresponding letter.

Passage one

There Is No Place like My Home[3]

NW: 361 GL: 7.9 AWL percentage: 3.73% Keywords: home; unique; decoration

There is no place like my home. My home is a welcoming and secure environment that is perfect for both entertaining guests and just a quiet night of pure relaxation. My home is a place where I find myself feeling safe and loved. The interior and exterior of my home is very unique, because my dad designed it, and I am very grateful to live where I do.

As I cruise down Riverton Drive I pass by my old high school, James River. Before turning onto my street, just ahead is the entrance to Robious Landing Park where I spent a lot of my childhood memories. Winding down my peaceful street I reach my residence. As

---

3 From StudyMoose website.

I pull into the beautiful cobblestone drive-way, I always admire the unique formation of my home.

The exterior of my home is all brick and the yard is <u>landscaped</u> with beautiful trees and shrubs. As I get out of my car, I routinely make my way to the back door, walking under the tangle vine arbor onto the stone patio[4].

The patio is made for outdoor gatherings and has comfortable furniture to lounge on. It also has a large stone fireplace and a grill for barbeque. My favorite part about my backyard is our garden, where we grow fresh fruit and vegetables to eat.

The sudden aroma[5] of my home smells of cinnamon[6] and is always comforting. My living room consists of my dad's favorite leather chair, a substantial love seat, a delightful cream colored couch, and a 64-inch flat screen TV.

This is where my family and I like to take a load off after a long day. If I had to describe my home's theme, it would be fall mainly because of its tasteful decorations and calming color scheme. All of the creams, browns, and reds make it that way.

My home not only symbolizes my family and me as people, but it also holds many memories. I am very lucky and internally grateful to have such a safe and nurturing place of residence and such a loving family to share it with. There's no place like my home.

1. **Why does the author think his house is unique?**

   A.   Because the home is full of safety and love.

   B.   Because there is a welcoming and peaceful air about it.

   C.   Because the home is designed by the author's father.

   D.   Because the author is very grateful to live there.

2. **Where will the author pass when he cruises down the Riverton Drive?**

   A.   Robious Land Park.

   B.   A cobblestone drive-way.

   C.   James River.

   D.   A peaceful street.

---

4 patio: 露台；天井

5 aroma: 芳香

6 cinnamon: 樟属的树，肉桂；肉桂皮

3. What does the underlined word "landscaped" (Line 1, Para. 3) mean?

A. Decorated.

B. Painted.

C. Equipped.

D. Crowded.

4. What can we learn from the author's description of his home?

A. The author's father makes furniture himself.

B. There is a cream crouch in the patio.

C. The theme of the house is summer.

D. They can eat what they grow in the garden.

5. How does the author feel about his home?

A. Home is only a place to live.

B. Home is priceless and irreplaceable.

C. It will be better to have a bigger home.

D. The memories from home are not important.

Passage two

My Sweet Home[7]

NW: 431 GL: 8.6 AWL percentage: 2.34% Keywords: sweet; nostalgic; togetherness

"There is nothing in the world as sweet as a home". As the saying goes, "East or west, home is the best". Home is the symbol of human togetherness—a place where all of us learn the first steps of life. For most people the very thought of home brings fond memories, nostalgic feelings and sad emotions.

My home is situated in a suburb called Gandhi Nagar[8] the capital of Assam. I was born in this city although my parents have migrated to the place due to service and occupation.

---

7 From Share Your Essays website.

8 Gandhi Nagar: 甘地纳加尔，位于班加罗尔

As for me, I feel a part and parcel of the city and consider it as my hometown. The locality where I live falls within the periphery of Guwahati[9] Club, one of the major commercial centres of the city and is noted for its educational institutions, sports facilities and green surroundings. My house is only a few yards from this commercial centre. The area is inhabited mostly by government servants, high-ranking officials and bureaucrats.

My house is situated at the side of a bye-lane leading to Guwahati club. It is a two-storied building constructed by my father about ten years ago. The top floor has been rented out. The ground floor, which we use, has four bedrooms, a drawing room part which also serves as a dining room, a kitchen and a bathroom.

My brother and myself share a room, while a room has been given to my elder sister. The third room which is the largest room in the house is used by our parents while the fourth room is kept as a guest room. All the living rooms have floor carpets, while the drawing room where we entertain our guests and watch TV has marble floor and an artistically carved showcase. The showcase contains numerous trophies, beautiful mementos and several attractive handicraft exhibits.

The house has a little porch in front where my father keeps his car. The portion between the porch and the road is used for gardening, which is taken care of by my mother. There is a small patch of land behind the house which is used for cultivation of vegetables and for dumping of scraps and useless articles of the house.

My home is a happy home. We the children love our parents and they in turn do all they can to make our life cheerful, enjoyable and least burdensome. We care for each other and do our very best to make our home a happy and a sweet home.

1. **What does the underlined word "nostalgic" (Line 4, Para. 1) mean?**

A. Impressive.   B. Homesick.   C. Lonely.   D. Painful.

2. **What can we infer from Paragraph 2?**

A. The author's parents were born and grew up in Guwahati.

B. Gandhi Nagar locates in the centre of Guwahati.

C. The author lives in the centre of Gandhi Nagar.

D. It was because of the job requirements that the author's parents moved to Guwahati.

---

9 Guwahati: City of Eastern Astrology, City of Temples, Gateway of the North-East India 古瓦哈提（印度城市）

3. **What does the author think of Guwahati?**

A. It is a place of strong attachment for the author.

B. It is too commercial to be named as hometown.

C. Guwahati is as small as a parcel.

D. It is not more important than the author's home.

4. **What do we know about the author's house?**

A. There are five living rooms in the house.

B. The house is near the educational centre.

C. The house was built by the author's father a decade ago.

D. There are eight rooms on the ground floor.

5. **Where does the author's family treat their friends?**

A. In the living room.

B. In the dining room.

C. In the portion.

D. In the drawing room.

Reading Skills

Lexical Cohesion

A text is not a collection of lexical items or sentences at random. Instead, it must be semantically unified.

Cohesion is the grammatical and lexical relationship within a text or sentence. Cohesion can be defined as the links that hold a text together and give it meaning. There are two main types of cohesion: grammatical, referring to the structural content, and lexical, referring to the language content of the piece.

Lexical cohesion refers to the cohesive effect achieved by the choice of lexical items. English lexical cohesive ties, according to Halliday, fall into the following categories.

Repetition: It means the choice of the lexical item that is in some sense similar to the preceding one. It is the most direct form of lexical cohesion.

Synonym: As a lexical cohesive device, it refers to the co-occurrence of two or more synonyms or near synonyms.

Antonymy: It refers to the co-occurrence of two or more antonyms to create cohesion within a text.

Hyponymy: It refers to the co-occurrence of two or more lexical items which are either subordinates or in the general-specific relations with each other.

Meronymy: It refers to the co-occurrence of lexical items which are in a part-whole relations with each other.

Collocation: It refers to the association of lexical items that regularly co-occur.

Exercises

Please read the following paragraphs or sentences carefully and decide which form of lexical cohesion they belong to.

Paragraph 1

The word "**home**" is a many-faceted word that combines different ideas. **Home** is culture, religion, the place where you live, friends, relatives, neighbors, cuisine, personal objects and environment. **Home** should be the place where you feel safe, free and in the state of health and physical well-being.

Paragraph 2

However, international students do suffer a lot from this **psychological sickness**. When they lose at least one of these, they feel **homesick** and start to understand the meaning of the word "home".

They **bring back** warm memories about the childhood and family holidays. Even music and flavors may make them **think about** their home. Any person may **miss** home when he is away for educational reasons.

Paragraph 3

Being a form of love, it is associated with a **tree**, which has deep **roots**. You feel at home, you feel comfortable and at ease in the place you are.

Paragraph 4

As I **cruise** down Riverton Drive I pass by my old high school, James **River**.
The sudden **aroma** of my house **smells** of cinnamon and is always comforting.

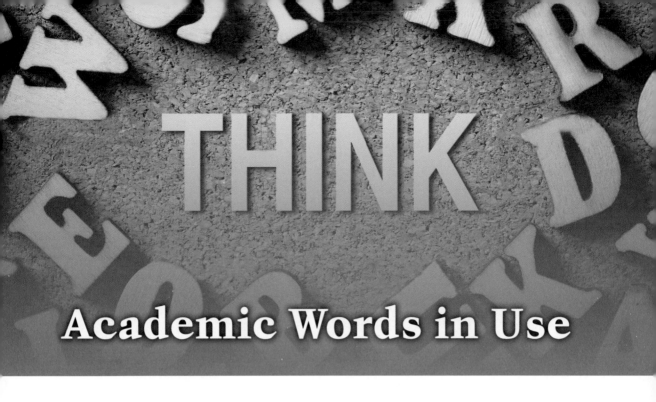

THINK

Academic Words in Use

Fill in the blanks in the following sentences with the appropriate words provided in the box below. Change the form of the words if necessary.

evaluate	cultural	eventually	symbol	mentally	aspect
generation	major	unique	isolation	affect	migrate

1. Drug abuse has long been a(n) _____ problem for the social safety.

2. _____, the army caught up with him in Latvia.

3. She was a woman of _____ talent and determination.

4. More than seven million people have been _____ by drought.

5. He was a beacon of hope for the younger _____.

6. Most birds have to fly long distances to _____.

7. Many deaf people have feelings of _____ and loneliness.

8. Don't _____ people by their clothes.

9. You may be physically and _____ exhausted after a long flight.

10. Do these _____ have any particular significance?

11. A rich and varied _____ life is essential for this couple.

12. Climate and weather influence every _____ of our life.

Writing

For this part, you are allowed 30 minutes to write an essay on the English saying, "East or west, home is best". You should write at least 120 words but no more than 180 words.

East or West, Home Is Best

Unit **6** On the Road

Viewing

Why Is Travelling Important?

About the video clip

This video clip discusses why travelling is important and introduces five benefits of travelling.

Understanding the video clip

Watch the video clip and fill in the blanks in the table below.

It is better to spend your money on experiences rather than on material things.	The memories you collect are _____. They will remain forever and will bring you more happiness than some new clothes or other material things. Think how good it will feel when you're old and you _____ see not only an ordinary routine but also adventures and unique experiences you had gone through. And not only when you're old, ever a few years from now, you can recall how much fun you had and plan your next adventure. In the end you will not _____ you've done but the things you didn't do.
It is a great opportunity to temporarily get away from your everyday life and look at it from a different point of view.	It's so much easier to deal with issues and _____ when you look at them from the outside. While travelling, you have a lot of time to think without distractions and _____. You will have a better perspective and maybe even realize these things are not that bad as you thought.

When you travel, you get out of your bubble.	In our everyday life we are used to doing the same things, meeting the same people, going to the same places. We basically live in our _____. You meet new people, other travellers and locals. You are exposed to _____. You see different landscapes and views. You experience new things. You learn that the world is diverse and it helps you understand people that are different from you.
Travelling actually makes you smarter.	You learn new things all the time. When you travel, you get into unusual situations and face different challenges. It makes you _____, handle things better, and come up with creative solutions. After all, the best way to learn is _____.
Travelling helps you to know yourself better.	You're out of your comfort zone and get to see your behavior in different situations, sometimes even extreme ones. You will _____ find out new things about yourself that you didn't know and decide what and how to improve. The best part of travelling is the people you meet along the way. You get to meet new people from countries around the world who you would never have met in your daily life. You listen to their stories. Tell yours, hear _____ and experience things together with people. Happiness is greater when shared with others.

Further thoughts

The prevalence of travelling has triggered a continuous wave of animated discussion over its benefits and drawbacks. List some of the drawbacks in the table below.

Drawbacks of travelling
1. It's expensive.
2. Flying leaves a big carbon footprint.

Banked Cloze

Below is a passage with ten blanks. You are required to select one word for each blank from the list of choices given in a word bank following the passage. Read the passage carefully before making your choices. Each choice in the blank is identified by a letter. Please write the corresponding letter for each item in the blanks. You may not use any of the words in the bank more than once.

Reasons Why Travel Was the Best Education[1]

NW: 257 GL: 8.5 AWL percentage: 3.28% Keywords: travel; learn; best

Travel was the best education. Here are four ways travelling increases your wisdom.

It 1. _____ your horizons. When you travel, it changes your perspective. Suddenly the world becomes about more than you or your country of origin. You will experience firsthand distant people and cultures rather than the narrow view sometimes provided through your 2. _____ media. And as you learn about other political, economic, and social structures, you will 3. _____ shift to a global view point where you understand how people and places are interconnected.

It helps you connect better with others. When you travel 4. _____, you gain a better

---

1 From Forbes website.

understanding of people and their actions. And over time, you begin to realize that despite our differences, we have more in 5. _____ than you would imagine.

It challenges you to grow. When you travel, you not only leave your hometown, you also leave your comfort zone. While that can be scary, it provides 6. _____ growth opportunities.

When you're in a land filled with a foreign 7. _____ and currency, exotic cuisine, and unexplored cities, you must move past your fear and immerse yourself into the unfamiliar. Use your curiosity to 8. _____ your adventures. Allow your courage to help you persevere through any travel 9. _____. And know that with a positive attitude, even getting lost in a strange place means you'll discover people and things you may have otherwise missed— and later be 10. _____ for the rich experience.

By learning about other people, places, and cultures, you'll also learn about yourself.

A) abroad	B) common	C) naturally
D) truly	E) broadens	F) resources
G) numerous	H) misfortunes	I) guide
J) local	K) strangely	L) grateful
M) narrows	N) language	O) hopes

Long Passage

You are going to read a passage with ten statements attached to it. Each statement contains information given in one of the paragraphs. Identify the paragraph from which the information is derived. You may choose a paragraph more than once. Each paragraph is marked with a letter. Please answer the questions by writing the corresponding letter after the statements.

Backpacking for Beginners[2]

NW: 933 GL: 7.3 AWL percentage: 2.63% Keywords: backpack; hike; destination

A   Backpacking is an adventure that blends hiking with backcountry camping. It lets you broaden your horizons beyond the car campground to enjoy a richer, more immersive outdoor experience. A key distinction from day hiking is the size of your pack—your backpack and you must carry all of life's essentials on your back. And you must choose those essentials with care.

B   To get ready for your first backpacking trip, follow these steps. Choose an easy destination: Short overnight hikes close to home are best. Get essential gear and clothing: Borrow and scrounge gear to save money. Plan your food: Just-add-water meals can be found at your local REI[3], or find easy to cook options at regular grocery stores. Also pack

---

2 From Rei website.

3 REI: Recreational Equipment, Inc. 美国户外用品连锁店

plenty of snacks for trail fuel.

C   If you have an experienced backpacking friend who knows you well, invite them along and they can be your guide. But you can also do this backpacking thing on your own—that's the focus of this article. We advise you to bring a friend regardless of their backpacking knowledge, though, because that makes any trip safer and more fun.

D   We've slept in our share of hostels and can offer some advice on ways to stretch your dollars in our "budget travel tips" article. Choose an easy backpacking destination. The key advice here is to err on the side of easy. If the hike is too hard, it can make for a miserable experience. If it's too easy, then you simply have more time to explore the area around your camp.

E   Follow these tips when you decide where to go backpacking for the first time. Consult with experienced backpackers: Hiking club members and REI store staff love to make trip recommendations. Hiking guidebooks are a valuable tool—you'll find the best selection for a given area in local REI stores and other local outdoor retailers.

F   Pick a place close to home. You want to spend more time hiking than driving. You also want to have ample daylight hours to reach camp before dark. Just a few miles round trip is fine. Plan on shorter distances than your typical day hike because walking with a heavier pack is slower and more difficult.

G   Aim for a few hundred feet of elevation gain. If you've hiked much, then you know that mileage alone doesn't tell the full story. So also choose a trail with less elevation gain than your typical day hike. Pick a well-traveled trail and well-established camp. It's nice to have hikers and backcountry campers nearby who can give you a hand if you run into difficulties.

H   Make sure there's water near camp. If your source will be a lake or large river, you should be fine. Streams and springs can dry up, though, so double check with local land managers before relying on a small water source.

I   Seek summer weather. Unless your destination is one where extreme heat or fire danger can be an issue, go in mid-summer to maximize daylight hours and your odds of comfortable conditions. Always check weather forecasts and don't hesitate to cancel or turn back if a storm moves in.

J   Consider "walk-in" campgrounds: Some state and national parks have campgrounds that are within a mile or so of a car campground. Staying in one of them is an excellent way to transition into backpacking.

K   Get essential backpacking gear and clothing. Keep your initial investment low by borrowing or renting the priciest items—your tent, sleeping bag and pad. Because they must fit you well, boots, and to a lesser extent packs, need to be your own personal gear. Because you have to carry and fit it all into your pack, backpacking gear has to be lightweight and compact.

L The following are essential items you'll need for any backpacking trip. Plan to share because a two-person tent weighs less and is more economical than two one-person tents. Bring a tent rated for three seasons (spring, summer and fall) rather than a four-season tent because you're not ready for mountaineering just yet. Learn more by reading "How to Choose a Backpacking Tent". You can also check out our guide to the best backpacking tents.

M Backpack: If you do borrow a pack, try it on first to be sure that it fits comfortably. Load it up with assorted items to about 30 pounds, and take it out on a long test hike. If it's comfortable on the hips and in the shoulders, it's probably fine for this first backpacking trip. If you decide to buy a pack, have an REI pack specialist measure your torso so they can properly fit you. Don't be tempted by an ultralight model for your first backpack because it will be less padded and have a less supportive structure than a more deluxe model. If you're determined to minimize weight, look first at ultralight tents, sleeping bags and sleeping pads. Learn more by reading "Backpacks: How to Choose". You can also check out our staff picks for the best backpacks.

N Sleeping bag: If you decide to buy a bag, consider the pros and cons of down fill vs. synthetic fill, especially in terms of the weather conditions you're likely to encounter. For your first bag, synthetic is a good choice because it's versatile and generally more affordable than down.

1. Take a friend with you for a backpacking trip for safety and fun. ☐

2. Cancel the backpacking trip if there will be a storm. ☐

3. Choose an appropriate sleeping bag according to the weather conditions. ☐

4. Choose a campground where you could get water easily. ☐

5. Ask the experienced backpackers for advice to decide where to go backpacking for the first time. ☐

6. In order to spend more time hiking than driving, choose a place near home. ☐

7. Load your backpack up with items to about 30 pounds to test whether it fits comfortably. ☐

8. Backpacking is an immersive outdoor experience which combines hiking with camping. ☐

9. It would be better to choose an easy destination than having a hard hiking. ☐

10. You may get some help when needed if you pick a trail and camp frequented by hikers and campers. ☐

Short Passages

There are 2 passages in this module. Each passage is followed by some questions or unfinished statements. For each of them there are four choices marked A, B, C, and D. You should decide on the best choice and mark the corresponding letter.

Passage one

How to Travel and Eat Your Way Around the World[4]

NW: 346 GL: 8.1 AWL percentage: 3.20% Keywords: travel; taste; food

The beauty of travelling the world is that you can home in on the things you are most curious about or the themes that bring you joy. For many people, this means adventure or volunteering or climbing as many mountains as possible.

For me, it means eating my way around the world and learning about food. I never started out this way. I planned my travels to last one year, expecting to return to my lawyering job in New York in 2009. After saving up as much as I could, I started "Legal Nomads" to document whatever adventures came my way. I never thought that I would be still writing years later, and certainly did not expect to have written a book about food.

---

4 From Nomadicmatt website.

Somewhere between Mongolia and China, I figured out that what I ate would become more of a focus for my travels. Growing up, food was never a big part of my life, but as time went on and I began to travel, it was obvious that my destination choices and daily schedules were planned around my taste buds. Moreover, I wanted to travel so that I could learn about what people ate and why. It wasn't just about the enjoyment of a meal or two but went much deeper.

How was it that these tastes and traditions that fascinated me came together to form the historical backdrop for countries I was only beginning to explore? Food was a never-ending source of wonder (and delicious meals).

But for those who want to do what I do, there are some valid concerns. How do you eat safely, without getting sick? What do you need to pack before you go that helps you on your tasty travels? And what do you need to know to build out an itinerary based around food?

I just wrote a book *The Food Traveler's Handbook*, answering these questions and more, and Matt asked me to post my thoughts here about how I eat the world.

1. **What is the beauty of travelling the world for the author?**

A. Adventure.

B. Volunteering.

C. Climbing as many mountains as possible.

D. Eating around the world and learning about food.

2. **What was the author's job before writing a book about food?**

A. A tour guide.　　B. A lawyer.　　C. A freelancer.　　D. A hiker.

3. **What is a reason for the author to plan his destination and daily schedules around food?**

A. He has been studying the history of food.

B. He plans to write a book about food.

C. He enjoys challenging his taste buds.

D. He wants to know what the locals eat and why.

4. **What does the underlined word "valid" (Line 1, Para. 5) mean?**

A. Reasonable.　　B. Absurd.　　C. Strange.　　D. Rare.

5. **One of the author's aim to write the book *The Food Traveler's Handbook* is to let the readers know _____.**

A. how to find the cheapest dining place.

B. what to pack before taking a tasty trip.

C. how to explore the unfamiliar places.

D. what to avoid in a route based around food.

Passage two

Backpacking in South America—A Beginner's Guide[5]

NW: 324　GL: 8.9　AWL percentage: 3.17%　Keywords: Chile; continent; America

South America is a continent like none other. I traveled there for nine months, and it was nothing like I had imagined.

South America is notorious for crime, and the situation can be mostly attributed to the poor financial and political conditions in some parts of the continent. The entire continent is not unsafe and need not be avoided. Having said that, let me tell you that bad incidents happen everywhere, and we should be careful and avoid dangerous places.

Out of the 14 countries, I visited Bolivia, Chile, and Peru during my nine-month solo travel in South America. In that entire time, I have only one bad incident when delinquents snatched my mobile while I was travelling in a bus in Santiago. Except for Santiago, a city

---

5　From On My Canvas website.

full of robbers and petty thieves, and Valparaiso, I felt safe in all the destinations in all three countries. No one ever harassed me or tried to loot me.

Now amongst the rest of the South American travel destinations, Brazil and Venezuela are unstable and unsafe. Mostly because these two have been in a political turmoil.

People had told me that the safest country in South America is Chile, and I felt so, too. Safety is coupled with financial security, and Chile is economically stronger than a lot of other countries. The south of Chile was so safe that we never even thought much before taking a walk or going to a nearby shop alone at night.

South America isn't any different from many other countries and continents in terms of safety. Please don't let anyone tell you that South America is a bad place and that it's entirely unsafe.

Use your judgment, ask your hotel for their safety advice, read about the local scams, and follow the common safety norms you follow in any new countries while travelling around South America, too.

1. **What does the underlined word "incidents" (Line 4, Para. 2) mean?**
   A. Events.　　B. Accidents.　　C. Changes.　　D. Chances.

2. **Why is South America notorious for crime?**
   A. There are a lot of robbers and petty thieves.
   B. Some places there suffer from poor financial and political conditions.
   C. The continent is very loose with laws and regulations.
   D. There is a large number of population who have no jobs.

3. **Which country is the safest according to the author's experience?**
   A. Bolivia.　　B. Peru.　　C. Chile.　　D. Brazil.

4. **What does the author think of South America in terms of safety?**
   A. It's a bad place and it's entirely unsafe.
   B. It's different from many other countries and continents.
   C. The entire continent needs to be avoided.
   D. The safety norms needed there are the same as those in any new countries.

5. **What is the author's attitude towards a trip to South America?**
   A. Disgusted.　　B. Objective.　　C. Indifferent.　　D. Sympathetic.

Reading Skills

Guessing Meanings According to Signal Words

Guessing meanings according to signal words helps you to capture the meanings of the unfamiliar words you're reading. Here are some guidelines for guessing meanings according to signal words.

1. **Definition**

   e.g.: Inflation means a rise in the general level of prices you pay for things you buy.

   an unfamiliar word: inflation

   signal word: means

   the definition: a rise in the general level of prices you pay for everything you buy

2. **Restatement**

   e.g.: The surface of Africa consists mainly of plateaus, or large flat areas, although these occur at different levels.

   an unfamiliar word: plateaus

   signal word: or

   meaning: large flat areas

3. Punctuation marks

e.g.: The use of computers to handle text, or word processing, was foreseen in the 1950s.

an unfamiliar phrase: handle text

signal punctuation marks: , ,

meaning: word processing

4. Examples

e.g.: Use navigation buttons, such as the "Next" button, the "Previous" button, the "Menu" button, and the "Exit" button, to go back and forth or jump to other topics while you are using your English software.

unfamiliar words: navigation buttons

signal words: such as

meaning: buttons on computer program that are used for turning on pages

5. Contrast

e.g.: Although Dara and Vipa are very close friends, they are very different. Dara spends a lot of money to buy things while Vipa loves to economize.

an unfamiliar word: economize

signal word: while

meaning: to use less money

6. Similarity

e.g.: Indonesia is producing Ford cars and trucks. Soon, Thailand and Vietnam will be producing the same products with, no doubt, the same quality.

signal words: the same products

Exercises

Please read the following sentences and guess the meanings of the underlined words according to the given signal words. Put down the Chinese accordingly.

1. When you're in a land filled with a foreign language and currency, <u>exotic</u> cuisine, and unexplored cities, you must move past your fear and immerse yourself into the unfamiliar.

Similarity signal word: foreign

exotic: _____

2. Get essential backpacking <u>gear</u> and clothing. Keep your initial investment low by borrowing or renting the priciest items—your tent, sleeping bag and pad.

Examples signal words: tent, sleeping bag, pad

gear: _____

3. <u>Backpacking</u> is an adventure that blends hiking with backcountry camping.

Definition signal word: is

backpacking: _____

4. Jack is <u>indecisive</u>, that is, he can't make up his mind.

Restatement signal words: that is

indecisive: _____

5. Most of them agreed; however, I <u>dissented</u>.

Contrast signal word: however

dissent:_____

6. A person or thing beyond comparison, a model of excellence, is knows as a <u>paragon</u>.

Signal punctuation marks: , ,

paragon:_____

THINK

Academic Words in Use

Fill in the blanks in the following sentences with the appropriate words provided in the box below. Change the form of the words if necessary.

benefit	economic	expose	perspective	encounter	legal
challenge	currency	diverse	option	unique	despite

1. Observers are worried about the possible _____ effects.

2. I'm a firm believer in the _____ of exercise.

3. Your core identity is what makes you _____.

4. Plants became increasingly _____ to adapt to the changing seasons.

5. WTO offers _____ as well as opportunities.

6. Students have the _____ of studying abroad in their second year.

7. The country experienced a foreign _____ shortage for several months.

8. Strong _____ safeguards are needed to protect the consumer.

9. He was publicly _____ as a liar and a cheat.

10. _____ the unsettled weather, we still had a marvellous weekend.

11. I think I have a very different _____ when it comes to the definition of what is beauty.

12. Every day of our lives we _____ major and minor stresses of one kind or another.

Writing

For this part, you are allowed 30 minutes to write an article about travelling according to the following three points. You should write at least 120 words but no more than 180 words.

Travelling

1. People who like travelling have their reasons.

2. Those who dislike travelling have their reasons as well.

3. In practice, travelling does more good than harm.

Viewing

7 Facts on the INFJ Personality Type

About the video clip

This video clip talks about a personality type called INFJs[1] and discusses the 7 fun secrets revealed about INFJs.

Understanding the video clip

Mark the boxes in the second column in the table if you think the seven fun facts of INFJs mentioned in the video clip surprised or impressed you and write down your reasons in the third column.

---

1 INFJ stands for Introvert, Intuition, Feeling, and Judging. The INFJ is one of the 16 personality types according to the theory of Katharine Briggs and Isabel Myers.

Facts about INFJs	The facts that impressed you	Reasons why the facts impressed you
1. They're magical unicorns!		Only one to two percent of the world's population are identified as INFJs.
2. They put the book in bookworm!		
3. They know how to climb the social ladder.		
4. They see things and understand them.		
5. They love a good puzzle!		
6. They're classy AF!		
7. They make routine unboring.		

Further thoughts

Imagine that you have a good friend who happens to be an INFJ. Then, based on the seven interesting characteristics of the INFJ, how will you get along with this friend? What can or can't you do with this friend? List some of them in the table below.

Cans	Can'ts
1. Read books together, whether it's history, Hogwarts or psychology.	1. Go to a party in a noisy bar together.

Banked Cloze

There is a passage with ten blanks. You are required to select one word for each blank from list of choices given in a word bank following the passage. Read the passage carefully before making your choices. Each choice in the bank is identified by a letter. Please write the corresponding letter for each item in the blank. You may not use any of the words in the bank more than once.

Escaping Your Comfort Zone, Regardless of Your Personality Type[2]

NW: 264 GL: 8.3 AWL percentage: 3.02% Keywords: comfort zone; psychological; growth

Have you ever heard of comfort zone? A comfort zone is a(n) 1._____ and physical place where comfort stops people from growth. When it's time to grow or to do something different, the comfort zone whispers, "Are you cozy enough? If no, step back into this place and relax." But growth rarely happens in the comfort zone. Personal growth always 2._____ that you step into the 3._____ and the inexperienced.

It is our personality traits that 4._____ our comfort zones, but we can use our knowledge of who we are to get away from the comfort zone. We're all about growth,

---

2 From 16 Personalities website.

and knowing your personality traits can help you know where your growth edge is. With this knowledge, you can 5._____ your strength and weakness.

Let's look at some examples. We hope they give you some ideas for making yourself a little uncomfortable.

- An introverted person might go to a business cocktail 6.____, even though they'd rather be home with a bowl of popcorn and their favorite reality show.

- An extroverted person might go to a weeklong silent retreat to get more in 7.____ with their inner selves.

- A thinking person might 8.____ a therapy group to help them discover their feelings through mindful body scans and heartfelt reactions from the group.

- A feeling personality type might take a critical-thinking course that helps them sort out what is subjective and what is 9.____ in their thinking.

Breaking free of the zone is an individual effort, so make it 10._____ yours. Outside of the zone, there is often a treasure of opportunities for self-development.

A) touch	B) psychological	C) challenging
D) uniquely	E) react	F) objective
G) balance	H) join	I) unknown
J) silence	K) define	L) comment
M) demands	N) strangely	O) party

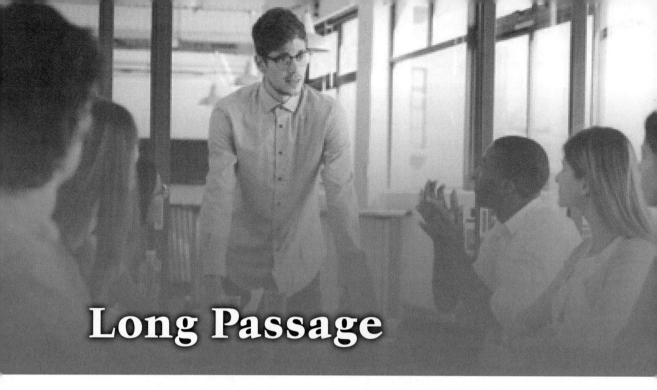

Long Passage

You are going to read a passage with ten statements attached to it. Each statement contains information given in one of the paragraphs. Identify the paragraph from which the information is derived. You may choose a paragraph more than once. Each paragraph is marked with a letter. Please answer the questions by writing the corresponding letter after the statements.

Ways Even Introverts Can Be Leaders at Wok[3]

NW: 958 GL: 8.8 **AWL percentage:** 4.31% **Keywords:** introvert; leader; inspiration

A   Kristi Hedges[4] has spent 25 years working with leaders to help them develop the skills necessary to lead their teams. And, introverts have been included in her training with just as much success as others!

B   In Hedges' latest book, *The Inspiration Code*[5], she says there's no natural-born leader, so introverts are on the same playing field as extroverts. In fact, you'd probably

---

3 From *Reader's Digest* by Amy Boyington.

4 Kristi Hedges: 一位高级领导力教练，专长于执行沟通，并且是亚马逊畅销书《激励准则》的作者

5 *The Inspiration Code*:《激励准则》，该书解密了有关于领导者如何有效交流、如何激励员工的技巧，旨在开拓人们的视野，引领大家走向未来

never guess that some famous people are introverts. We talked to Kristi about some of the skills introverts already have and how they can change them into leadership skills in the workplace.

C　　In the first place, good listening is an important skill for leadership. An introvert person feels more comfortable listening than speaking. Although this sounds like a problem for someone who wants to be a leader, it's a very helpful skill to have.

D　　Introverts tend to think first and speak second. They're most comfortable going inward with their ideas before introducing them. Their quieter nature can make them easier to get long. They're also comfortable giving a conversation space, and can be more adept at fully focusing on the person in front of them. Consider your listening skills an asset, and make them work to your advantage. Taking everything in and processing it before speaking will make sure that your messages are thoughtful and based on right information.

E　　Strong observation and absorption abilities are also required by leaders. An introverted person who finds it difficult to communicate with others can develop more comfort speaking through observing.

F　　"Introverts are less concerned with talking just to talk, and therefore, when they do share something it's already well-developed," Hedges says. "Introverted leaders tend to be observers, as well. They notice the little differences that others may miss. They are often the ones who can tell you what's really going on in a situation." Observation skills not only help an introvert take in information, but they can also help introverts focus on what other people do when communicating.

G　　Make mental notes of effective communication strategies others use in meetings and work on mirroring those in your communications. Successful leaders use these methods daily to help them stay on top of their game.

H　　Furthermore, a good leader always has a plan. Introverts may feel anxious in meetings, often waiting for the right moment to jump in with their ideas. Instead of waiting, Hedges suggests that it's better for introverts to think ahead and have a plan. Challenge yourself to put your ideas on the table in the first few minutes, and then get your voice in the room. The plan of the meeting is set early, and by speaking then, you're establishing yourself as an active participant.

I　　Even though an introvert may have a quieter personality than an extrovert, he or she can still encourage others with the leadership. How? Hedges says it all comes from success. "Introverts motivate by being successful on their own terms and communicating what they're doing," she says. Introverts take up between one-third to one-half of the population, so it stands to reason that many introverts are leaders, or want to become leaders. "Role-modeling what leadership looks like as an introvert breaks down stereotypes and motivates others to pursue their own goals," Hedges says.

J　　To be a leader, the introverts must focus on his or her core values. To be successful in leadership, it's important that introverts start viewing their weaknesses as strengths. That means focusing on the values that you most want to show in the presence of your team. "Write down a list of your top personal values, and narrow them down to a list of five core values," Hedges recommends. "This can help you to be clear about what's most important for you to convey." Show confidence and commitment—and that will do the same job.

K　　One of the biggest challenges that introverts face is to feel comfortable in social situations. They may find it hard to find new ways to connect with their team members because connection often means socialization. Fortunately, Hedges says it's okay to let your team into your world if that's what makes you feel most comfortable. "Invite the team to do something that you would enjoy, like bringing in a catered lunch where you can casually talk. Or if you're a sports fan, have a team-building session at a game. If you're relaxed and enjoying the moment, you'll do a far better job," she says.

L　　Remember, getting more comfortable being uncomfortable is a way to leadership. It all depends on your willingness to change current behaviors so you can become more at ease in anxiety-causing situations. According to Hedges, "What feels comfortable can change with practice. If you push yourself to try new behaviors, such as speaking in public, after some time it will become easier. What was once an uncomfortable behavior becomes part of your usual practice."

M　　Once you begin to master the art of speaking out and realizing that you can be a powerful leader, start making your presence known to your team. "Introverts can spend a lot of time in their heads thinking ahead and putting plans together. This is a good skill to have, but other people can't see all that work being done," Hedges says. "Teams want to see and understand what their leaders are focused on, so you'll do everyone a favor if you learn to show your thoughts, values, and plans even if they aren't finalized yet. Make an effort to let your team members know what's important for you, and what you're thinking about."

N　　These inspirational suggestions may give you the boost you need to continue to strive to be your best self in the office.

1. Before introducing their ideas, introvert people will think about their ideas inwardly.

2. An introvert person likes listening because he/she feels more comfortable

with just listening.

3. There is no natural-born leader, so introverts have equal chances to be leaders as extroverts.

4. Introverts must focus on their core values and convey them to their teams.

5. Many introverts are or seek to be leaders because one third to one half of the population are introverted.

6. Introvert people are good at observing, and they only share something well-developed.

7. Introvert leaders should learn to show their thoughts, values, and plans to the team even if they aren't finalized yet.

8. It's better for introverts to have a plan before a meeting so that they can establish themselves as active participants.

9. It's okay for introvert leaders to let the team into their world so that they will feel more comfortable.

10. More practice will make uncomfortable behaviors become comfortable.

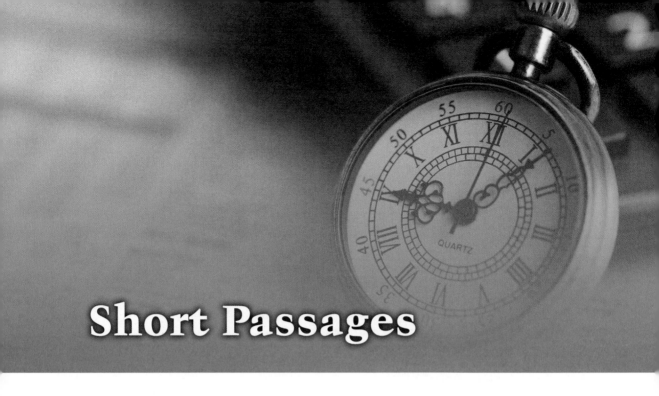

Short Passages

There are 2 passages in this module. Each passage is following by some questions or unfinished statements. For each of them there are four choices marked A, B, C, and D. You should decide on the best choice and mark the corresponding letter.

Passage one

A Procrastination Short Story and the Rebel Within[6]

NW: 371 GL: 6.9 AWL percentage: 2.35% Keywords: procrastination; intention; action

This is a short story about procrastination. If you're prone to procrastination, I think you'll find something in it that you've never thought about before.

Jane looked like a desperate fugitive on the run from coursework completion. Dark under-eye circles, energy utterly drained—and that was just me after listening to her for a whole hour.

She had two weeks to complete her degree thesis. The culmination of three years of study, the key to her chosen career—and was she getting down to it? No.

6 From Self Hypnosis USA website.

As she told me bitterly of her obsession of procrastination: "I'm a rabbit caught in headlights!"[7]

That's what procrastination feels like. The intention is there but the action isn't. "Inactivity is the grave of good intentions," as I think someone once got around to saying.

Indeed, Jane was a professional procrastinator. "I work hard at not working. I have engaged myself in my social activities, started singing lessons, found new TV shows to watch. I'm doing everything but what I should be doing."

"I know what will happen! I'll get to the point where not doing it will feel much worse than the thought of doing it, then I'll cram it into the last couple of days. Mark, why do I procrastinate?"

Good question. Why do we procrastinate?

Well, "conditioned rebellion" plays a part. As kids we're told what to do:

"Get to bed now!" I don't want to!

"Eat your food!" I don't want to!

"Finish your assignment!" No!

We can become used to feeling reluctant when it comes to stuff we have to do.

This automatic "rebellion" can slide into adulthood. Sure, Jane had chosen to do her degree, but she still felt as if she "had to do it". I always loved reading but at school, I would not read novels on the English curriculum ("on principle"), only ones I'd chosen.

Procrastination isn't just about laziness. We all want to control stuff in our lives, and procrastinating can be an unconscious attempt to do things on our own terms. But it doesn't work, because procrastination leaves us feeling less in control.

The next time you catch yourself procrastinating, reflect on whether you might just be rebelling against…what?

---

7 "I'm a rabbit caught in headlights!": This idiom means that someone is so frightened or nervous that he/she does not know what to do.

1. How long has Jane been studying to get her degree?

A. Two weeks.　　B. Three weeks.　　C. Two years.　　D. Three years.

2. What does the author mean by saying "Inactivity is the grave of good intentions" (Para. 4)?

A. Good intentions are meaningless without actions.

B. Actions are meaningless without good intentions.

C. Actions will always lead to good intentions.

D. Good intentions will always lead to actions.

3. What did Jane do in order not to work?

A. She worked hard on her degree thesis.

B. She started singing lessons.

C. She found old TV shows to watch.

D. She engaged herself in volunteering activities.

4. According to the author, why do people procrastinate?

A. Because they are conditioned to put things off since childhood.

B. Because laziness is in the nature of everyone.

C. Because they are reluctant to do what they are forced to do.

D. Because people tend to rebel against themselves.

5. What suggestion does the author give to people who tend to procrastinate?

A. Work hard instead of being lazy.

B. Do things on their own terms.

C. Think about what they might be resisting.

D. Have some control of their lives.

Your Attitude Counts, Not Your Age[8]

NW: 383　GL: 7.8　AWL percentage: 3.92% Keywords: attitude; ambition; courage

Once there was a small kingdom named Paradium bordering to another kingdom. There was peace and harmony everywhere as the king believed in non-violence.

As for every good story there is a bad story: A powerful and notorious kingdom prepared to attack Paradium. Paradium came to know about the attack, but was helpless due to its weak army. After all, the soldiers never participated in battles. For soldiers, fighting was only an art, and it was not meant for killing anyone. They used their fighting skills for maintaining internal peace and harmony in the civil society.

The soldiers of Paradium were less in number, and had no capacity to fight against their enemy. The ministers advised king to gather all the men above the age of 18 years to participate in the battle. The king had no choice, but to accept ministers' advice to counter the threat posed by invading enemy. There was a boy named Dave who had ambition to join the army.

When this matter was brought in front of the people of Paradium, Dave thought that this was an opportunity to accomplish his ambition. When Dave approached General Grefeld and unveiled his ambition, the first question the General asked Dave was about his age. Dave said that he was 15 years old. General asked, "What will you do in the battle?" Dave replied, "I will fight until my last breath." General laughed and said, "You are just a kid!" Dave looked into the eyes of General and said confidently, "Nobody cares whether I am a kid or not. Everyone's aim in battle is to kill the opponents and defend the country."

"Great!" said the General, and he was impressed with the Dave's answer. The General said, "Dave, be right next to me during battle. You will become a good warrior one day."

Dave played a crucial role in the battle. When the General was about to be checkmated by enemies, Dave drew his sword and pierced into the enemies who were ready to capture the General. He killed 20 people through his bravery by braving risk

---

8　From Mrkhyd's Weblog website.

to his life, and saved the General. Finally, Paradium won. The General appreciated Dave's ability and courage, and realized his wrong estimation. Hence, what counts at the end is your attitude, not age.

1. Which is part of the reason why the soldiers of Paradium were weak?

   A. The soldiers had little battling experience.

   B. The soldiers didn't want to be killed.

   C. Fighting was just an art for the soldiers in Paradium.

   D. It was unnecessary to fight in peaceful and harmonious Paradium.

2. What did the ministers of Paradium suggest to the king?

   A. They suggested that the soldiers should become good warriors.

   B. They suggested that the soldiers should fight until their last breath.

   C. They suggested that all men above the age of 18 participate in the battle.

   D. They suggested that the soldiers fight to maintain internal peace and harmony.

3. Why did General Grefeld agree to Dave joining the army despite Dave's age?

   A. Because Dave would be a good soldier.

   B. Because Dave was courageous and determined.

   C. Because Dave promised to save General Grefeld's life.

   D. Because Dave was talented in fighting against the enemies.

4. What does the underlined word "checkmated" (Line 2, Para. 6) mean?

   A. Cornered.   B. Followed.   C. Cheated.   D. Injured.

5. What qualities made Dave a victory in the battlefield?

   A. His intelligence and power.

   B. His youth and energy.

   C. His ambition and luck.

   D. His ability and bravery.

Reading Skills

Guessing Meanings According to Word Formation

Whenever you read extended texts in English, you will come across words which you do not know. Your instinct is probably to look up the unfamiliar words in a dictionary. If you do this for each word, it will take you a great deal of time. You therefore need to develop strategies for dealing with unknown words.

There are two questions to ask yourself whenever you meet an unfamiliar word. The first question is, "Do I need to know the meaning of the word?" If not, you can keep reading and ignore the word. The second question you need to ask is, "Is an approximate meaning enough?" If not, you need to look up the word in a dictionary.

If the answers to both questions above are "no", it means you can guess what the word means and then keep reading. Sometimes the formation of the word (i.e. prefix, suffix, root) will help you guess an approximate meaning.

"How can affixes help me understand new words?" Affixes can help you because they don't change in meaning. A lot of difficult English words are built out of smaller pieces: a main part (the root) and a collection of prefixes and suffixes. Root carries the basic meaning of the word, prefix changes root's meaning, and suffix part of speech. By breaking them down into parts, one can try to guess the general meaning of them.

Consider the following sentence:

In Hedges' latest book, *The Inspiration Code*, she says there's no natural-born leader, so introverts are on the same playing field as extroverts.

The words you want to guess in this sentence are "introvert" and "extrovert". Both of these words can be divided into two components respectively: "intro-" and "extro-", which are the prefixes; "-vert", which is the root. You can get the following information by analyzing the word formation:

"Intro-" is a Latin prefix meaning "inwards".
"Extro-" is also a Latin prefix meaning "outwards".
The root "-vert" comes from Latin "vertere" which means "to turn".

As a result, "introvert" refers to a person who tends to turn from social contacts and become preoccupied with their own thoughts, while "extrovert" refers to a person concerned more with practical realities than with inner thoughts and feelings.

Exercises

Divide the underlined words below into different parts (roots, prefixes and suffixes). And then combine the meaning of each part to find the meanings of the words. An example has been given.

1. The plan of the meeting is set early, and by speaking then, you're establishing yourself as an active participant.

2. They may find it hard to find new ways to connect with their team members because connection often means socialization.

3. Teams want to see and understand what their leaders are focused on, so you'll do everyone a favor if you learn to show your thoughts, values, and plans even if they aren't finalized yet.

4. Inactivity is the grave of good intentions.

5. This automatic 'rebellion' can slide into adulthood.

Word	Prefix	Root	Suffix	Part of speech	Meaning
unacceptable	un	accept	able	adjective	not acceptable
participant					
socialization					
finalize					
inactivity					
adulthood					

THINK

Academic Words in Use

Fill in the blanks in the following sentences with the appropriate words in their proper forms. Change the form of the words if necessary.

focus	strategy	challenge	motivate	professional	reluctant
participate	maintain	pursue	approach	appreciate	estimate

1. You can't fully _____ foreign literature in translation.

2. The new advertisement _____ really helped to boost production.

3. My cat felt _____ when taking a selfie with me.

4. He is determined to go abroad to _____ his further study.

5. Only by keeping down costs will our company _____ the competitive advantage over other companies.

6. He is using his camera to _____ on the flower which is to be photographed.

7. Be careful how you _____ her—she's very hot-tempered.

8. The worker _____ the price of house decoration yesterday.

9. They expected him to _____ in the ceremony, but he didn't show up in the end.

10. After watching the _____ baseball game, Johnny aspired to become a famous athlete one day.

11. This discovery _____ traditional beliefs and changed people's way of life.

12. Understanding these effects will _____ you to try even harder to do your part to protect our planet.

Experience vs. Personality

Writing

For this part, you are allowed 30 minutes to read the following paragraph and continue writing to make a well-structured article. You should write at least 120 words but no more than 180 words.

Which Determines Your Personality, Genetics or Life Experience?

As some reports say, "The characteristics of us naturally have much more effect on our personality than other experience that we have in our life."

_____

_____

_____

_____

_____

Unit  Let's Get Social

Viewing

Building Social Connections

About the video clip

If you just moved to a new city and did not have any friends there, what would you do to get connected with others? This video clip introduces the appropriate ways to build connections with others.

Understanding the video clip

There are various ways to have better connections with others. Put a tick (√) in the right column if it is mentioned in the video clip. An example has been given.

Ways to get better connected with others	Mentioned
1. Get out and explore his new neighborhood.	√
2. Visit a bike shop to see if there are neighborhood bike groups.	
3. Call 211 if you need a little more help.	
4. Write your ideas down and pick one thing you can do for your neighbor.	
5. Be open to accept help when it is offered and help others in return.	
6. Go for a walk with your new co-workers.	
7. Spend time by yourself watching TV or on your computer most of the days.	

Further thoughts

Social connections are central to our well-being. Building social connections offers various benefits. List at least five points in the table below.

Benefits of building social connections
1. Building social connections can enhance your sense of happiness.

Banked Cloze

Below is a passage with ten blanks. You are required to select one word for each blank from the list of choices given in a word bank following the passage. Read the passage carefully before making your choices. Each choice in the blank is identified by a letter. Please write the corresponding letter for each item in the blanks. You may not use any of the words in the bank more than once.

Let's Get Social: What Does That Really Mean?[1]

NW: 245 GL: 8.3 AWL percentage: 2.83% Keywords: like; get social; network

For many people, they began their careers never having logged onto the Internet, not worrying about the "Like" button, and they certainly did not imagine that there would be thousands of social networks online. And a "social engagement" was something you put on your calendar—an event with peers where you went somewhere.

You may be 1._____ to give "getting social" an honest try, but adding a computer keyboard to that with no other explanation. After you jump in and see how fast things move, and 2._____ all of the social platforms you could be on, you shift into overwhelming.

You get this feeling in your stomach like you've been sent to the headmaster's 3._____

---

1 From searchenginepeople website.

for being late to school for the fourth time, and your 4._____ expressions might even mimic that scene. Have you felt like that?

First, it's 5._____ too much for social media and online marketing professionals to use the words, "Let's get social," without explaining what that means. It could be 6._____ to expect that everyone knows how to socially engage via their keyboard and 7._____.

Second, brace yourself! "Engaging" means doing more than clicking "like" on platform. Social media is all about two-way dialogues, building 8._____, and being part of conversations.

That is a fair start. Most 9._____, being social online means sharing others' stuff more than you share your own. Sending out only your marketing messages 10._____ broadcasting, and that is not social. You also need to listen.

A) mouse	B) importantly	C) facial
D) willing	E) expecting	F) relationships
G) office	H) discover	I) equals
J) unreasonable	K) able	L) strangely
M) small	N) wishes	O) working

Long Passage

You are going to read a passage with ten statements attached to it. Each statement contains information given in one of the paragraphs. Identify the paragraph from which the information is derived. You may choose a paragraph more than once. Each paragraph is marked with a letter. Please answer the questions by writing the corresponding letter after the statements.

When to Unfriend vs Unfollow a Friend or Colleague on Social Media[2]

NW: 1,061 GL: 8.5 AWL percentage: 3.67% Keywords: unfriend; unfollow; social media

A   There's a lot of middle ground on social media between "friends who share everything" and "mortal enemies"—here's how to clean up your feed without feeling bad.

B   Social media gets a lot of attention for the "media" part. After all, who doesn't love seeing pretty pictures, funny memes, and interesting videos? However, when it comes to the effects on your real-world life, you need to be paying just as much attention to the "social" part. Facebook, Instagram, and "the like" are just as much about relationships as they are about information, says Diane Gottsman, national etiquette expert.

---

2 From *Reader's Digest* by Charlotte Hilton A.

C   When everything works well, social media is a great tool to connect with like-minded others, maintain good relationships, and have fun. As anyone who's ever spent any time on the sites knows. However, things can take a turn for the worse, fast. Social media can do really weird things to your mind. All it takes is a racist uncle, a work conflict, or opposing views on an upcoming election to turn your fun feed into a nightmare. But before you give up social media for good, you have a few tools at your disposal to clean up your feed.

D   Just like in the real world, there are a lot of relationship levels between "people who share everything with each other" and "sworn enemies", and social media tools can help you sort out exactly how much engagement you want to have with each "friend", Gottsman says.

E   Knowing the difference is one thing; knowing how to use these tools is another thing. But it's an essential skill for handling the most awkward social media situations. Don't worry, we've got you. Here are some common social media situations along with advice for the proper etiquette in handling them.

F   Unfriend: A neighbor keeps badgering you to host a "party" for the makeup she sells. Social media has become the method of choice for people in multi-level marketing business to hawk their wares and expand their down-lines. But no matter what they're selling, the bottom line is that their posts are self-serving. "These friends see you as a way to make money and are using your relationship with them to that end," Gottsman says. If you like the products, it's not a problem but if you feel overwhelmed by their requests simply unfriend them, she says. "If it's a really close friend, talk to them in person first about how it makes you feel and then unfriend if they don't respect that boundary," she adds.

G   Unfollow: Your boss, current or former. Even if you're on great terms with your boss, it's a best practice to keep your work and personal life separate and not be friends with him or her on social media, Gottsman says. However, if you're already friends then it might harm your working relationship if you suddenly unfriend them. Thus, unfollow them can be a middle ground, she says. If you insist on being friends with colleagues, make sure you know what your social media profile is really saying about you.

H   Unfriend: Your super fit friend who sends you into a shame spiral. Comparison is the thief of joy, and nowhere is the old adage more true than on social media. If you can't stop looking at a celebrity's or friend's pictures, as well as envying their lives or bodies, then it's time to unfriend. And don't forget that much of what you see on social media is an illusion anyhow.

I　　Unfollow: Your college roommate posts 20 pictures a day of her new baby. Even people who love seeing pictures of cute babies, kids and pets, it can be hard to match the zeal of the proud parent. In particular, the one who enjoys posting every burp or bark to social media. While this can get annoying, your friend isn't technically doing anything wrong or offensive and she'll likely move out of this phase eventually, at which point you may want to re-follow her, Gottsman says. Unfollowing will give you a covert breather.

J　　Unfollow: Your mom who comments on every single post she reads. Social media works by showing you not just posts from your friends but also their activity. For example, what they've liked, commented on, or purchased. This can really clog up your feed with unnecessary information if you're friends with people who like or comments on every single thing they see. Simply unfollowing will clear the clutter while still allowing you to maintain an online relationship with your mother, Gottsman says. "This way you can look at her posts and comments when it's convenient for you and limit the time you spend on it," she says.

K　　Unfriend: That one person you're hate-following. Social media should be about finding things that uplift and inspire you yet sometimes it's tempting to "hate follow" someone. Whether it's a celebrity, a political figure, or an old classmate that you love to loathe, this type of social media relationship can be very toxic. "If someone is taking up too much space in your mind or you're spending a lot of time looking at their page, then it's time to unfriend," she explains.

L　　Some people hesitate to use the unfollow or unfriend tools out of fear of hurting someone's feelings. Don't worry, you can let this one go. Most time they won't even notice you've done it, Gottsman says. The apps don't notify people when they are unfriended or unfollowed, and most people have too many friends to worry about checking their lists, she says. Understand that unfriending someone doesn't mean you don't like them; it just means you are drawing a boundary on social media and sometimes that can even be better for the relationship.

M　　There's one last tool you need to know about it: The block user function. Unfortunately some people use social media to stalk, harass, bully, intimidate, coerce, or otherwise hurt and manipulate. If you find yourself in a situation that feels unsafe for any reason, don't hesitate to use the "block" function, Gottsman says. Not only will this unfriend a person but it will prevent them from sending you future requests or messages or even seeing your profile. You can also use the "report" feature to let Facebook or Instagram know if the person is breaking the rules of the platform.

1. Social media tools can help people engage with each "friend" to the exact level they desire. ☐

2. Concerns about others' feelings cause some people not to use the "unfollow" button. ☐

3. It's time to unfriend someone if he/she is occupying too much of your mind space or your time. ☐

4. People should pay as much attention to the "social" part of Facebook, Instagram, and "the like" as their "media" part. ☐

5. It's time to unfriend if you can't cease looking at a friend's pictures, as well as envying their lives or bodies. ☐

6. Social media can lead you away from fun and into a nightmare really fast. ☐

7. You can look at your mother's posts and comments at your convenience when you have unfollowed her. ☐

8. It's time to unfollow someone who posts dozens of pictures a day of a baby or a pet. ☐

9. It's appropriate not to be friends with your boss on social media. ☐

10. A friend who keeps bothering you to buy the cosmetics she sells is crossing the boundary. ☐

Spread Kindness

Short Passages

There are 2 passages in this part. Each passage is following by some questions or unfinished statements. For each of them are four choices marked A, B, C, and D. You should decide on the best choice and mark the corresponding letter.

Passage one

How to Break the Ice and Meet New People[3]

NW: 345   GL: 8.1   **AWL percentage:** 3.31%   **Keywords:** comment; break; fact

Tired of the same old opening lines? We've all heard them, and they can sometimes be a real turn-off. But since you never get a second chance to make a first impression, what's said in those first few moments is as significant as it often is tongue-tying. If you're one who stumbles and falls—during those initial moments when you're meeting someone new, you've come to the right place. And if you think you're a smooth operator who's known for witty opening lines, there may be something here for you to learn, too.

Break the ice by making a comment or statement, often followed by a question. This

---

3 From Reader's digest website.

technique works especially well when you're with a group of people sharing a similar experience, such as waiting at the doctor's office, attending a gallery opening, or standing in line.

You can also make comments about your surroundings. Or, say something more personal. By making statements about surroundings or events, you establish a common bond that readily and easily promotes dialogue.

Facts are entertaining and interesting and can be great ways to break the ice at social and business events. You can use anything and everything from the weather to things about your city to current events. Little tidbits can be intriguing and a good way to get the banter going. Make sure you know your facts, however, or someone else could correct you, which could be embarrassing. Unless, of course, your intention is to spark a conversation with a little bit of controversy!

Cliches are used so frequently because they're effective and because they usually work well. You can use them just about any time, at any place from nightclubs to parties to business functions. You can always make a joke of using a cliche, such as "I can't believe I'm actually going to say this, but do I know you from somewhere?" In all cases, be honest and sincere. The saying goes that what you say isn't as important as how you say it.

1. **What does the underlined word "witty" (Line 6, Para. 1) mean?**

A. Stupid.

B. Humorous.

C. Careful.

D. Critical.

2. **What can we learn from the second paragraph?**

A. Sharing opinions with a group of people can help you make new friends.

B. It's easier to make a first impression on strangers by asking questions.

C. Making a comment to break the ice works effectively when waiting at the doctor's office.

D. It's a great way to start a conversation by asking questions in all situations.

3. **What could be a great way to break the ice?**

A. Sharing facts about current events.

B. Gossiping on your neighbors.

C. Shaking hands with others.

D. Giving others a big hug.

4. **What is the reason for using cliches to break the ice?**

A. Because they're so traditional that everyone can use them well.

B. Because they can easily establish a common bond.

C. Because they're effective and usually work very well.

D. Because they will spark a conversation with a little bit of controversy.

5. **What is the author's attitude towards using a cliche?**

A. Critical.

B. Objective.

C. Indifferent.

D. Supportive.

Smiling Really Is Contagious and Here's Why[4]

NW: 370 GL: 7.8 AWL percentage: 3.26% Keywords: communication; research; smile

Smiling is one of the ways that we communicate with the world. Smile and the whole world really does smile to you. At least, that's according to the results of a recent study.

Picture the scene: You're walking down the street, minding your own business when a stranger passes you by. They don't say anything at all, but they do give you the smallest, briefest smile. In an instant and almost unwillingly, you're doing the same thing. You just can't help it!

In honor of World Smile Day, it's time we get some real answers on this very pressing matter. With all this grinning going on in the world, it really does beg the all-important question: Is smiling contagious?

Well, according to a study, the answer could well be "yes". As part of the research, some social psychologists looked into why we often mimic the facial expressions of our peers when we talk to them. Interestingly enough, one of the results that the researchers drew was that we "try on" the emotions of others when we are communicating with them. So, when a friend tells us some gleeful news and looks happy and joyful, we may unconsciously display the same emotion through our facial expression. In doing so, we have a chance to feel and understand their emotions.

So, the reason we smile when someone smiles at us is that we want to feel the same way as that person. It is through this small social kink that we're able to have a deep level of communication with the people around us.

However, this is not the case for everyone out there. Those with Central Core Diseases, who cannot accurately mimic others' expressions, often have a problem with this level of communication. Although they can recognize when someone is smiling at them, they are not always able to offer the same expression back.

Since facial expressions make up a large portion of our communication, they are very important in social dynamics and can help us to build relationships and bonds with others.

---

4 From *Reader's Digest* by Charlotte G.

So, the answer to the question "Is smiling contagious?" is most certainly "yes". If you've yet to crack a grin on this World Smile Day, go ahead and spread the joy!

1. **What does the underlined phrase "can't help" (Line 4, Para. 2) mean?**
   A. Desire.
   B. Endure.
   C. Stop.
   D. Insist.

2. **Why do we often imitate the facial expressions of others according to social psychologists?**
   A. Because we are good at mimicking facial expressions of others.
   B. Because we hope to make friends with them.
   C. Because we want to sense the emotions of others in this way.
   D. Because we would like to leave a good impression on them.

3. **What is the effect of "trying on" the emotions of others?**
   A. We can prove to others our sincerity.
   B. We can have an in-depth communication with them.
   C. People laugh at you when you give smiles to the strangers in a park.
   D. People get angry when a stranger passes by and says nothing at all.

4. **What is true of the people with Central Core Diseases?**
   A. They are able to offer a similar facial expression back.
   B. They cannot recognize a smile when someone is making one.
   C. They are able to have a deep communication with others.
   D. They are unable to accurately display the same expression.

5. **What is the author's suggestion to the readers?**
   A. Influence others with your smile.
   B. Smile to yourself.
   C. Learn how to smile.
   D. Change your mind about smiles.

Reading Skills

Guessing Meanings According to Meaning Relations

Meaning relations are those relations that constitute conceptually viable elaborations or associations of linguistic contents expressed in words. In other words, meaning relations are those that are instantiated by conceptually constrained associations of a set of given words. In terms of reading skills, guessing meanings according to meaning relations refers to guessing meanings based on synonyms and antonyms as context clues.

Synonymy is a meaning relation which involves two or more expressions having the same interpretation. Synonymy will always mean one of two or more words in the English language which have the same or very nearly the same essential meaning.

Antonymy is a meaning relation which involves two or more lexicons having opposite interpretations or meanings.

Example

Guess the meaning of the underlined word from the context.

I had been young, healthy, and smug. She had been old, sick, and desperate. Wishing with all my heart that I had acted like a human being rather than a robot, I was saddened to realize how fragile a hold we have on our better instincts.

Clue: Compare the words "old, sick, desperate" to "young, healthy, smug". The word "old" is the antonymy of "young"; the word "sick" is the antonymy of "healthy". Therefore, we can indicate the word "smug" is the antonymy of "desperate".

Exercises

Choose the right answer by guessing the meaning of each underlined word from the context.

1. Social media should be about finding things that uplift and inspire you yet sometimes it's tempting to "hate follow" someone.

   A. reduce   B. encourage   C. respect   D. prefer

2. There's a lot of middle ground on social media between "friends who share everything" and "mortal enemies"—here's how to clean up your feed without feeling bad.

   A. competitors   B. members   C. families   D. fighters

3. While this can get annoying, your friend isn't technically doing anything wrong or offensive and she'll likely move out of this phase eventually, at which point you may want to re-follow her.

   A. outstanding   B. comfortable   C. terrible   D. sick

4. You can also make comments about your surroundings. Or, say something more personal.

   A. distance   B. neighborhood   C. location   D. religion

5. If you're one who stumbles and falls—during those initial moments when you're meeting someone new, you've come to the right place.

   A. hesitates   B. crawls   C. confuses   D. staggers

THINK

Academic Words in Use

Fill in the blanks in the following sentences with the appropriate words in their proper forms. Change the form of the words if necessary.

media	communicate	network	comment	joyful	research
expert	embarrassing	display	establishing	social	similarly

1. The online service is designed to help home buyers and sellers _____ via mobile devices.

2. The two buildings are _____ on the whole.

3. We have _____ trade ties with these regions.

4. The actress revels in all the attention she gets from the _____.

5. The Internet is a worldwide computer _____.

6. Some _____ show us when and why the following things HR should replace.

7. He tried to hide his _____ by telling jokes.

8. Illegal behavior is no longer _____ acceptable.

9. I feel unqualified to _____ on the subject.

10. My uncle is a(n) _____ in repairing radios.

11. He had an opportunity to fully _____ his talents.

12. She brought _____ to countless people through her music.

Writing

For this part, you are allowed 30 minutes to read the following sentences and write a well-structured article. You should write at least 120 words but no more than 180 words.

Many people believe that the increasing use of the cell phone in people's life has a huge negative impact on both individuals and society. Do you agree?

My Opinion on the Increasing Use of the Cell Phone

Appendix: Video Script, Key and Sample Answers

Unit 1　A Brand-New Start

Video script

Welcome to Stanford

NW: 528　GL: 7.9　AWL percentage: 3.05%　Duration: 2′36″　WPM: 203

I remember when I was a freshman coming to Stanford. I, was pretty jittery. I was really nervous. And I was just thinking, wow, I do not know anybody out here. And that can be pretty intimidating.

Stanford was just like the great unknown. No one in my family had gone to college so there was no preparing for a college speech. What it meant to live in a room with a stranger you don't know. I was scared about whether or not I'd fit in, or whether my personality, my temperaments or the things I like to do would be the Stanford norm or would have a place at Stanford.

I think the new student orientation is about beginnings, discovering self, discovering others, discovering who you want to be in this next phase of your life.

New student orientation begins the year here at Stanford. And so it's when all of the new students move in on the same day, and they go through a series of activities together that bond them as a class.

NSO's important because I met my upperclassmen mentors who really shaped my Stanford trajectory. And they really made sure I felt at home and comfortable my first week at Stanford.

When you come into Stanford you meet a lot of people. So you might meet someone your first day and they might be become your best friend for all four years.

When, a great part about new student orientation, everyone arriving as everyone's getting settled in their dorms, there's this real sense of dorm life and dorm pride.

At our foundation, we are about relationship, faculty member to student in a research project or even relationship in the collective.

In a whole dorm community, in an athletic team, all of that, to say we're not about competing at the expense of one another but instead raising each other up. This was a place that I found I could really count on everyone else around me to, like, have my back.

And so when you start talking to other people you really realize, oh man, like, everyone else is feeling just the same as I and you just kind of move past the initial nervousness and you really build a community and a home of... of that.

Welcome, students, we are so glad you're here. You are joining a family. When we say family, we mean a family.

I want to encourage you to embrace this place and embrace its perfection and imperfection. To think about where you want to leave your fingerprints and what kind of legacies you want to leave but also get your sense that this is your big, beautiful place. This is your home.

Key and sample answers

Viewing

Understanding the clip

1.T   2. NG   3. T   4. F   5. T   6. T

Further thoughts

Expectations	Nervousness
Making new friends.	Dorm life.
Joining a variety of associations.	Building a community.
Taking part in clubs and organization.	Assignments and tasks.
Forming a study group.	College rules and norms.
Taking CET 4, CET 6...	Homesick and cultural shock...

Banked Cloze

1–5 IABMF 6–10 CNGKE

Long Passage

1–5 DEHJA 6–10 BFiGL

Short Passages

Passage one 1–5: ABCDD
Passage two 1–5: DBCAD

Reading Skills

Reference answer 1: orientation, freshmen, campus, parents

Reference answer 2: When it comes to leisurely activities, you'll have many choices.

Reference answer 3: You may attend various sessions and take part in activities like parties, sport competitions and games. Orientation gives students the opportunities to quickly adapt into the new college life.

Academic Words in Use

1. via   2. leisurely   3. maintain   4. accurate   5. eventually
6. focus   7. affectionately   8. lecture   9. mental   10. virtual
11. facilities   12.community

Writing

Sample writing

How to Succeed in College

There are some basics or fundamentals that enhance success in college.

First of all, be in class and take notes. Being on time and keeping good attendance are important. If students are not in class, then they are not learning what is being taught. It is also important to pay attention when in class and take notes where necessary. Reviewing notes several times will enhance information to get into your long-term memory so that it will not be forgotten.

Secondly, take pride in yourself and your work. Do quality work. If something is worth doing, it is worth doing well.

Thirdly, set educational and other goals. This will give you a purpose for going to school and it provides self-motivation. Remind yourself why a good education is wanted and what achievement is made in college.

To sum up, these useful tips will help you to avoid failure and to become successful in college.

Unit 2   College Education: East and West

Video script

How the American Colleges Lift Students Out of Poverty

NW: 554 GL: 8.3 AWL percentage: 4.86% Duration: 3′30″ WPM: 158

Elite universities love to market themselves as engines of upward mobility. Elite and egalitarian. And for low income students they do offer incredibly generous financial aid. "I found out that for a family like ours, we wouldn't have to worry about affording Harvard." "I'm really grateful because I wouldn't have been able to get here, were it not for the amazing financial aid package I received."

Thanks to some new economic data, we can now see just how good these colleges actually are at lifting students out of poverty. And when we do, the results aren't what you'd expect.

A group of economists looked at two sets of records: Income tax forms from the IRS and graduation data from the Department of Education with all the identifying information taken out. They looked at 10.8 million people born between 1980 and 1982. The tax forms showed how much money their families made. And the researchers placed each person in a group based on that income. From the bottom 20%, whose families made about $25,000 or less per year, to the top 20%, whose families made about $110,000 or more per year. They looked at where each person went to college and how their position on the income ladder changed about 10 years after graduation. If you look at kids from the bottom 20% who go to elite colleges like Harvard, they do really well. Over half of them go from families in the poorest fifth of the American economy, to being in the top fifth by the time they're in their mid-thirties. Same thing at Stanford, Yale, and Princeton. The problem is, these schools don't let in very many kids from the bottom rung of the ladder. In the class of 2013 only 4.5% of Harvard students came from the bottom 20% of the income distribution. So, about a fourth as many people as you would expect if Harvard were representing the American population. Testing data show there are plenty of qualified low income students out there. They're just not applying to elite schools. Many, many, many more people who were born into privilege and have wealthy families get to go to these places.

Then there are colleges with the opposite problem, like Moultrie Technical College in Georgia. Thirty-four percent of their students came from the bottom rung of the ladder. So, it's really good at access, but a very small fraction of them make it to the top fifth of the income distribution.

But there are some schools who are good at both. Cal State LA—it's a commuter school. It's enrolling a lot, a lot, a lot of poor kids. Twenty percent of students come from the bottom rung of the ladder and half of them end up at the top rung. PACE University in New York, which does a little worse on access—ten percent of its students come from the bottom rung of the ladder. But, well, over half of them wind up in the top 20%. David Leonhardt at *The New York Times* refers to them as America's Great Working-Class Colleges. And, I really like that saying that they're not the famous ones, they're not the ones that get a lot of press coverage or get represented in movies. There's no "Social Network" about Cal State LA. But, they're doing the work.

Key and sample answers

Viewing

Understanding the video clip

Colleges	Data	Results
Harvard	Over <u>half</u> of them go from families in the poorest fifth of the American economy, to being in the top <u>fifth</u> by the time they're in their mid-thirties. In the class of 2013 only <u>4.5%</u> of Harvard students came from the bottom 20% of the income distribution.	The kids who go to <u>elite</u> colleges do really well, but plenty of qualified low income students are not <u>applying</u> to these school.

Moultrie Technical College	<u>34%</u> of their students came from the bottom rung of the ladder.	It's really good at <u>access</u>, but a very small fraction of them make it to the top fifth of the income <u>distribution</u>.
Cal State LA	<u>20%</u> of students come from the bottom rung of the ladder and <u>half</u> of them end up at the top rung.	David Leonhardt at *The New York Times* refers to them as America's Great <u>Working-Class</u> Colleges. They are not the famous ones but they're doing the work.
PACE University	<u>10%</u> of its students come from the bottom rung of the ladder, but well over <u>half</u> of them wind up in the top <u>20%</u>.	

Further thoughts

Yes	No
1. Low income families cannot afford tuition of those elite universities.	1. Funding and students loans can reduce the financial burden of impoverished families.
2. Students from wealthy families have privilege for better educational resources.	2. Students from poor families have more motivation to work hard and change life.
3. Students without financial burden have less opportunities to explore interest and cultivate competitive skills.	3. Independent students tend to face the hardships in studies with more persistence and diligence.
4. Money is a necessity to participate in elite programs and study tours to expand your horizons and knowledge.	4. Impoverished students take on more responsibilities at home and therefore value learning opportunities more.

Banked Cloze

1–5 DGAOB 6–10 JFKEM

Long Passage

1–5 HECKF 6–10 BDJIK

Short Passages

Passage one 1–5 DCCDC

Passage two 1–5 CAAAB

Reading Skills

Paragraph 1: EAP courses can also be in-sessional courses.

Paragraph 2: Hangzhou is chosen to set up a top-class research university due to its connection to Mr. Shi and the enthusiasm of its government.

Paragraph 3: Be strategic in your course choices.

Academic Words in Use

1. strategic   2. institutions   3. academic   4. assess   5.major

6. innovative   7. dimensions   8. credits   9. maturity   10. evaluation

11. lecturer   12.document

Writing

Sample writing

Why Do We Attend College?

Attending college can be a prodigious next step for someone freshly graduated from high school. A person with a college diploma gains more opportunities to earn higher income, and leads a more secure and successful life. Higher education meets the social demands for more powerful workplace. Yet college education brings more than career advantages.

Apart from knowledge development and skills cultivation, it is the place where many people find themselves and mold their future. College, for most, is a stepping stone into a successful adult life. Communication, cooperation and competition they learnt and experienced in college would be influential in their future life. Besides, persistency and responsibility can also be fostered when they are expected to solve problems independently.

Attending college also allows a person to make connections with a variety of people via organizations, clubs and parties. The environment supports young people to intercommunicate about literature, goal of life, art and emotions which are hard to be talked about after graduation. They tend to socialize and make friends with some people who might be their life-long friends.

In short, college education is crucial to prepare a person for future career and life.

Unit 3　Fashion

Campus Style: What Does Your Style Mean to You?

NW: 599　GL: 9.0　AWL percentage: 4.28%　Duration：3′40″　WPM: 163

Joshua Susie: Hi, this is Nadim Joseph.

Nadim Joseph: And I'm Joshua Susie.

Joshua Susie: And this is the first video edition of campus style.

Nadim Joseph: Follow us as we walk around campus and ask people what their style means to them.

Nadim Joseph: We're here with...

Sally: Sally.

Nadim Joseph: Hi, Sally. Okay, so, um, could you please tell us where your outfit is from?

Sally: All right. Today I'm wearing, um, this is Zaida, Topshop and Zaida and Zaida. I love Zaida. Actually, it's one of my favorite stores. When I go back home in Bahadin, actually, that's all. Like, that's where I shop from. And Topshop, Topshop's like my favorite store too.

Nadim Joseph: Cool, how would you describe your style?

Sally: My style has changed a lot over the years. I'm on my 4th year. Um, I would say I want more from like being, um, like formal to the dressing to like, just comfortable. Yeah, it's comfort.

Joshua Susie: Could you just let us know where you got your outfit from?

The man with earphones: Um, I think this jacket's from H & M. Um, I got these pants are from the flea market and I got my shoes from Urban Outfitters.

Joshua Susie: And how would you describe your style?

The man with earphones: Um, I would, I woud call it's really me, like it's more something between urban and maybe just as popular, I guess. Um, it really reflects kind of the way that, you know, I envision myself in the way I like to carry out myself.

Joshua Susie: Okay, so if you could just let us know where you got your outfit from?

The girl with scarf: Um, well, I got my jeans a couple years ago from American Eagle,

I think, and my top I think was Guess. I think that was it, and then this is from Chapters, but….

Joshua Susie: So how do you go about, like developing your own style?

The girl with scarf: Um, I don't know, I guess. I think the most prominent, like, aspect of my style would be my hair and that was the decision that I did over like a couple of years. Something that just felt right, something that's like really helped me express myself and like, stay true to the kind of person that I've wanted to be.

Joshua Susie: Do you use your style as a way to shape that how people perceive you? Is it kind of something that you use to kind of express your own individuality?

The girl with scarf: I think definitely everybody does. Um, I think that what you put out into the world is a reflection on your character in a way, and so by expressing positive vibes through what you're, how you're presenting yourself. I think that can really impact you and your relationships with other people as well.

Nadim Joseph: So where did you get your jacket in your outfit?

The last interviewee: Oh, well, I shop around all the time and I got my jacket at Holt Renfrew. Yeah, they're closing down in Ottawa and it's my college jacket. My shirt here is from H & M. I like their playing colored V-necks. My pants and my trousers are from Zara and so are my shoes.

Nadim Joseph: Nice! Thank you.

The last interviewee: Yeah.

Nadim Joseph: And what do you think your clothing has to say about you, in our respect?

The last interviewee: Well, I think everybody's style is very important in their daily life. It projects themselves what they think about themselves, but for me I think my current style says bold, um, uninhibited and ready to play.

Nadim Joseph: Nice! perfect! Thank you.

Joshua Susie: Thanks for tuning in for the first video edition of campus style. We hope you guys enjoy it.

Nadim Joseph: If you think you have what it takes to be in the next edition of campus style, contact us at artsacharlatan.ca.

Viewing

Understanding the video clip

Sally: B
The man with earphones: D
The girl with a scarf: A
The last interviewee: C

Further thoughts

My current style is urban. Dressing nicely is a pleasant thing to me and I enjoy that. If I dress well, I will feel confident about myself. My style is an attitude and a way of life. It is something that can shape my personality. Dressing in a proper and decent way could help me perform better. And it shows respect to people around me.

Banked Cloze

1–5 J A I C B   6–10 E G L K D

Long Passage

1–5 G B H D L 6–10 I F C K A

Short Passages

Passage one 1–5: B D B A C
Passage two 1–5: C B B D D

Reading Skills

Passage 1: During your education at college, it is very important to find your personal style because that will help you become a more confident person.

Passage 2: Perhaps this is why "looking sharp", as my father used to put it, was so important.

Academic Words in Use

1. insignificant 2. trend 3. approachable 4. invested 5. identified
6. survive 7. Traditional 8. somewhat 9. relaxed 10. interaction
11. freedom 12. fairly

Writing

Sample writing

Good and Bad Effects of Fashion on Students

Today's youths are totally influenced by new fashion trends. They tend to follow fashion styles in order to look different and stylish in front of others by wearing different types of clothes and accessories.

As we can see, there are good and bad effects of fashion on students. Fashion has become extremely important among students. These days, students are keen to follow the latest fashion to look smart and presentable. If you dress well, you'll feel good and more confident. However, too much of it can have a negative impact, especially on students. Some college students shop frequently to change their wardrobe and flaunt the latest trend. And they focus so much on fashion that they don't get sufficient time for other work.

It's good to keep yourself updated with fashion but if it interferes with your academic performance, it should be avoided.

Unit 4　Food Is Culture

Video script

What Breakfast Looks like Around the World

NW: 523 GL: 8.1 AWL percentage: 2.28% Duration: 3′39″ WPM: 143

No matter where you are waking up around the world, a hearty breakfast is the best way to start the day. From elaborate spreads to sweet and savoury bites, here's what breakfast looks like around the world.

Breakfast in Morocco is all about simplicity, such as bread and egg dishes. For those with a sweet tooth, Sfenj is a popular doughnut style treat. It is eaten plain or soaked in honey. Moroccan breakfast also doubles as teatime.

Shakshuka is a common breakfast dish eaten throughout the Mediterranean and the Middle East. The dish is made of eggs poached, baked or scrambled in a savoury tomato-based sauce, thought to have originated in Tunisia, then spread to Israel and the surrounding region by Jewish immigrants.

In England, a full English breakfast means little room left on your plate. Sometimes referred to as a "fry-up"—the plate features a sunny side-up fried egg, sausage, fried bread, bacon, beans and tomatoes, paired with a side of hot tea. Some locals might even add on mushrooms, black pudding and potatoes for the ultimate English breakfast.

A traditional Japanese breakfast includes an array of savoury bites. It often consists of miso soup, fish and steamed rice, usually served with egg. Natto, fermented soybeans mixed with soy sauce and mustard, is also eaten in the breakfast set.

A Filipino breakfast starts with sour, sweet and savoury flavours of Tapsilog. Thin slices of beef tapa are served with fried egg and garlic fried rice. The beef is often marinated in soy sauce, calamansi juice, vinegar, sugar and garlic.

While meals vary across the country, breakfast in the United States tends to include a few regular go-tos. Americans enjoy chowing down on eggs, bacon, sausage and starchy sides like toast or pancakes.

This South Asian dish Halwa Poori is beloved by people in both India and Pakistan. Poori, which is made out of wheat flour, is served deep fried with Chana Masala, a spicy chickpea curry, potato and sweet milk and semolina-based confection called Halva.

In Myanmar, sip on savoury Mohinga soup. This Burmese favourite is a rice noodle and fish soup with lemongrass, garlic and catfish. It is considered to be the national dish of Myanmar.

Breakfast in Turkey is an elaborate spread known as Kahvalti, which is a Turkish word for breakfast. It consists of fresh cheeses like feta and Kashkaval, black and green olives, fresh baked white bread, fruit preserves, honey, sweet butter and plenty of brewed black tea served in Turkish tea glasses.

Columbia Changua is a hearty soup made of milk, water, scallions and eggs. This soup is garnished with cilantro and topped with a piece of stale bread called Calado, which softens in the Changua.

In Bulgaria, Banitsa is a traditional flaky pastry eaten for breakfast. It is prepared by layering a mixture of whisked eggs and pieces of cheese between phyllo pastry and then baked in an oven. It can be eaten hot or cold.

Mas huni is a traditional breakfast dish in the Maldives. Tuna is combined with minced chilies, finely chopped onions, and freshly grated coconut. It is eaten with Roshi flatbread.

Key and sample answers

Viewing

Understanding the video clip

Matching

1. D 2. A, F, H 3. B, E 4. C 5. G

Fill in the blanks

Country or region	Iconic breakfast dish	Characteristics
Morocco	Sfenj	Breakfast in Morocco is all about <u>simplicity</u>.
The Mediterranean Region	Shakshuka	The dish features eggs <u>poached</u>, <u>baked</u> or scrambled in a savoury tomato-based sauce.
England	Full English breakfast	Having this dish means <u>little room left on your plate</u>.
Japan	Traditional Japanese breakfast	It includes an array of savoury bites.
Philippines	Tapsilog	A Pilipino breakfast starts with <u>sour</u>, <u>sweet</u> and savoury flavours.
The United States	Eggs, bacon, toast and pancakes	Breakfast in the US tends to include a few regular go-tos.
India and Pakistan	Halwa Poori	Deep fried Poori served with curry and Halwa.
Myanmar	Mohinga Soup	This dish is a <u>rice noodle</u> and <u>fish soup</u> with lemongrass, garlic and catfish.
Turkey	Kahvalti	Breakfast in Turkey consists of <u>fresh cheeses</u>, black and green olives, fresh baked <u>white bread</u>, fruit preserves, <u>honey</u>, sweet butter and black tea.
Columbia	Changua	A hearty soup dish made of <u>milk</u>, water, scallions and eggs.
Bulgaria	Banitsa	The dish is a traditional pastry.
Maldives	Mas huni	It is a traditional breakfast dish that uses <u>tuna</u>, chilies, onions and <u>coconut</u> as ingredients.

Further thoughts

Chinese breakfast dish	Characteristics
Pancakes (*Jianbing*)	It is an iconic Chinese breakfast from northern China and is arguably the "king of breakfast" in China. *Jianbing* is commonly wrapped around a deep-fried dough slice, and topped with ingredients like eggs, scallions, coriander and a savoury sauce.
Dim sum	Dim sum is extremely popular in southern China, especially in Guangdong Province. Dim sum includes a wide range of dishes like shrimp dumplings, spring rolls and porridge.
Soymilk and *youtiao* (deep-fried dough sticks)	A great combination of Chinese breakfast. Chinese people like to dip and soak *youtiao* in the soymilk and eat it after it absorbs the taste of soymilk.

Banked Cloze

1–5 FANIL 6–10 GBCMK

Long Passage

1–5 KDFGI 6–10 BJCEH

Short Passages

Passage one 1–5: BBDCD

Passage two 1–5: CDDAB

Reading Skills

1. The amount people eat and leave uneaten also differs from group to group. Some people from Middle Eastern and Southeast Asian countries might leave a little bit of food on their plates.

2. Like everyone else, Chinese people love fast food. Western salty, fatty fast-food chains such as McDonald's and KFC serve up vast quantities of lunch and dinner to the world's most populous nation.

3. Nevertheless, what is considered edible in some parts of the world might be considered inedible in other parts. The values or beliefs a society gives to cooking ingredients characterize what families within a cultural group will eat.

1. percent   2. classic   3. react   4. varies   5. immigrant

6. domestic   7. demonstrates   8. feature   9. minor   10. regional

11. inaccurate   12. source

Writing

Sample writing

My Favorite Chinese Food

Chinese cuisine originates in different regions of China and every ethnic group has its unique representative dishes. One dish that is extremely popular in China, especially in Sichuan Province, is Mapo tofu. It is also my favourite Chinese food.

Mapo tofu is a typical Sichuan dish. This dish was named after a spotted woman (pronounced as "Mapo" in Chinese) as that lady was famous for preparing delicious stir-fried tofu. Main ingredients used to make this dish are tofu, chili peppers, ground beef or pork, and Sichuan peppers. Authentic Mapo tofu is aromatic, flavourful, spicy and numbing. These characteristics make the dish stand out among others and help the dish gain popularity both in China and abroad. It is also said that a tour of China is incomplete without tasting this spicy Sichuan food.

Unit 5   East or West, Home Is Best

Video script

What Is Home

NW: 166   GL: 8.2   AWL percentage: 0   Duration: 1′44″   WPM: 96

Hey dad, what's home?

Home is...

You're restless, aren't you?

People say they live and die in the valley as if it's a bad thing.

Celebrities, cars, girls, speeches, family.

非常的祥和、宁静 (inside you, lives home)

[Music]

Don't worry, kid. It doesn't matter where you are. You've got everything you need right here.

Mommy still hold me when I was little. She's missed it, you know, your lab, could smell the salt in the head... feel it honors again.

Never read one, have you?

I believe that if you look for them, there are more wonders in this universe than you could ever imagine.

That's home to me.

Honestly, kid, no matter where I go, this always be home with me.

This is home.

Wherever you are, promise me, you just mean.

Home exists in you, take it with you and you'll always be home.

Key and sample answers

Viewing

Understanding the video clip

1. live and die; as if

2. celebrities; speeches

3. where you are; you need

4. more wonders; could ever imagine

5. no matter where

6. exists in

Further thoughts

Proverbs about home	Translations of the proverbs	Your understandings towards the proverbs
1. East or west, home is best.	金窝银窝，不如自己的草窝。	There is no place in the world better than one's own home.
2. Although the sun shines, leave not your cloak at home.	未雨绸缪。	Think of danger in times of safety and always be prepared for the worst.
3. Charity begins at home, but should not end there.	仁爱须由近及远。	If you want to pass your love to others, you should love the one around you firstly.
4. A book holds a house of gold.	书中自有黄金屋。	There is a wealth of knowledge in books. If you study hard, good things will come to you.
5. Home is home, though never so homely.	不如归去。	Your home will be there waiting for you.
6. Home is where the heart is.	家是心之所系。	One's home is made up of the places and people one loves or cherishes most.

Banked Cloze

1–5 HCODK   6–10 MIAEG

Long Passage

1–5 CEABL   6–10 JIMDG

Short Passages

Passage one 1–5: CCADB

Passage two 1–5: BDACD

Reading Skills

Paragraph 1: Repetition

Paragraph 2: Synonym

Paragraph 3: Meronymy

Paragraph 4: Collocation

Academic Words in Use

1.major   2.Eventually   3.unique   4.affected   5.generation

6.migrate   7.isolation   8.evaluate   9.mentally   10.symbols

11.cultural   12.aspect

Writing

Sample writing

East or West, Home Is Best

There is a general debate about where the best place for people is. Some people may think that golden hotels are best because we can enjoy a lot in it. But as far as I'm concerned, the best place is our home, as the saying goes: "East or west, home is best."

First of all, for me, in spite of the fact that I really like travelling, I always miss home during trips. My home is a little world where I can make my own rules and live according to them. Moreover, if we feel tired, the best place for us to go is home. We can talk to our parents or our lover about our difficulties. Last but not least, everybody has a home. This is the most private place for a person. People need safety and we feel safe in our homes. We can relax and forget about everything in this wonderful place. It is really important for everybody.

As stated above, when at home, problems tend to be slighter and smaller. Troubles seem to disappear and all difficult things may become easier. That's why home is the best for most of us.

Unit 6   On the Road

Why Is Travelling Important?

NW: 554 GL: 5.5 AWL percentage: 7.13% Duration: 3′16″ WPM: 170

We all need a break from our everyday life. Going on a vacation is fun and fulfilling. But you can gain a lot more by actually travelling, exploring and being present at the places you visit. Here are some benefits of travelling.

It is better to spend your money on experiences rather than on material things. The memories you collect are like treasures. They will remain forever and will bring you more happiness than some new clothes or other material things. Think how good it will feel when you're old and you look back to see not only an ordinary routine but also adventures and unique experiences you had gone through. And not only when you're old, ever a few years from now, you can recall how much fun you had and plan your next adventure. In the end you will not regret the things you've done but the things you didn't do.

TravelLing is a great opportunity to temporarily get away from your everyday life and look at it from a different point of view. It's so much easier to deal with issues and solve problems when you look at them from the outside. While travelling, you have a lot of time to think without distractions and make healthy decisions. You will have a better perspective and maybe even realize that things are not that bad as you thought.

In our everyday life we are used to doing the same things, meeting the same people, going to the same places. We basically live in our comfort zone. When you travel, you get out of your bubble. You meet new people, other travellers and locals. You are exposed to different cultures. You see different landscapes and views. You experience new things. You learn that the world is diverse and it helps you understand people that are different from you.

Travelling actually makes you smarter. You learn new things all the time. When you travel, you get into unusual situations and face different challenges. It makes you push your limits, handle things better, and come up with creative solutions. After all, the best way to learn is through experience.

Travelling helps you to know yourself better. You're out of your comfort zone and get to see your behavior in different situations, sometimes even extreme ones. You will be surprised to find out new things about yourself that you didn't know and decide what and how to improve. The best part of travelling is the people you meet along the way. You get to meet new people from countries around the world who you would never have met in your daily life. You listen to their stories. Tell yours, hear various opinions and experience things together with people. Happiness is greater when shared with others.

Travelling may sound scary or too challenging to some people. And it's OK. Just remember that you can choose your own kind of travel. It doesn't have to be trekking in the mountains, although that could be fun. But you can do anything. Explore cities, do some couch surfing, relax in nature, visit small villages and so on. You will get more confident and learn what is good for you. Have a nice trip.

Key and sample answers

Viewing

Understanding the video clip

It is better to spend your money on experiences rather than on material things.	The memories you collect are like treasures. They will remain forever and will bring you more happiness than some new clothes or other material things. Think how good it will feel when you're old and you look back to see not only an ordinary routine but also adventures and unique experiences you had gone through. And not only when you're old, ever a few years from now, you can recall how much fun you had and plan your next adventure. In the end you will not regret the things you've done but the things you didn't do.
It is a great opportunity to temporarily get away from your everyday life and look at it from a different point of view.	It's so much easier to deal with issues and solve problems when you look at them from the outside. While travelling, you have a lot of time to think without distractions and make healthy decisions. You will have a better perspective and maybe even realize these things are not that bad as you thought.
When you travel, you get out of your bubble.	In our everyday life we are used to doing the same things, meeting the same people, going to the same places. We basically live in our comfort zone. You meet new people, other travellers and locals. You are exposed to different cultures. You see different landscapes and views. You experience new things. You learn that the world is diverse and it helps you understand people that are different from you.
Travelling actually makes you smarter.	You learn new things all the time. When you travel, you get into unusual situations and face different challenges. It makes you push your limits, handle things better, and come up with creative solutions. After all, the best way to learn is through experience.

	You're out of your comfort zone and get to see your behavior in different situations, sometimes even extreme ones. You will be <u>surprised to</u> find out new things about yourself that you didn't know and decide what and how to improve. The best part of travelling is the people you meet along the way. You get to meet new people from countries around the world who you would never have met in your daily life. You listen to their stories. Tell yours, hear <u>various opinions</u> and experience things together with people. Happiness is greater when shared with others.
Travelling helps you to know yourself better.	

Further thoughts

Drawbacks of travelling
1. It's expensive.
2. Flying leaves a big carbon footprint.
3. There's no place like home.
4. There will be language barriers.

Banked Cloze

1–5 EJCAB   6–10 GNIHL

Long Passage

1–5 CINHE   6–10 FMADG

Short Passages

Passage one 1–5: DBDAB
Passage two 1–5: ABCDB

Reading Skills

1. exotic: 外来的，异国的
2. gear: 工具

3. backpacking: 徒步旅行

4. indecisive: 犹豫不决的

5. dissent: 不同意

6. paragon: 模范

Academic Words in Use

1. economic   2. benefits   3. unique   4. diverse   5. challenges

6. option   7. currency   8. legal   9. exposed   10. Despite

11. perspective   12. encounter

Writing

Sample writing

Travelling

People who like travelling have their reasons. They firmly believe that travelling can help them expand their scope of knowledge, especially in their geographical and historical learning. They go on to point out that touring will provide more chances for them to enjoy distinctive food and experience different lives that they otherwise cannot possibly have.

Those who dislike travelling have their reasons as well. They would argue that travelling means to spend a considerable amount of money and consume enormous energy. For example, traffic and accommodation require money spending while seeing sights often tires them.

In practice, travelling does more good than harm. If our finance and health permit, we might as well do some travelling from time to time. It will help us feel like our best self because we are more willing to receive the world's many lessons, whatever their shape or size. It helps us recognize our shared humanity with others and dissipate fear or misunderstandings. After all, it's much more fun to love the world than to be afraid of it.

Unit 7　Character Is Destiny

Video script

7 Facts on the INFJ Personality Type

NW: 459　GL: 7.3　AWL percentage: 6.13%　Duration: 2′48″　WPM: 164

Ever heard of the MBTI test? It's shorthand for Myers-Briggs Type Indicator[1].

First published in 1943, it still holds significance today and is used in many circumstances, ranging from marital counseling and relationship compatibility, to career selection and personal development.

As lovers of psychology and personality types, we thought it would be fun to do a series on all sixteen types. Today we'll be talking about INFJs, otherwise known as "The Advocate". Here are seven fun secrets revealed about INFJs.

One: They're magical unicorns!

Okay, not in a literal sense, but INFJs statistically have been reported as the rarest personality type. To be exact, only one to two percent of the world's population are identified as INFJs, with slightly more females than males. No wonder you're such mysterious creatures!

Two: They put the book in bookworm!

As introverts, INFJs love to pass time with the good old reading hour. They enjoy learning new things and have a broad range of interests, whether it's history, Hogwarts or psychology. If you find that your INFJ hasn't gotten back to your text, he might just be visiting platform Nine and Three-quarters.

Three: They know how to climb the social ladder.

Consider INFJs as the goats in society, they know how to climb a mountain when they see one. Ambitious, knowledge-seeking and always open to self-improvement—this type does what it takes to reach their goals. If they aren't careful, however, they may push themselves too hard!

Four: They see things and understand them.

Think of Charlie from *The Perks of Being a Wallflower* (《壁花少年》), a classic INFJ, or Holden Caulfield from *The Catcher in the Rye* (《麦田里的守望者》). The minute they walk into a room they can absorb everyone's moods.

Five: They love a good puzzle!

1　The Myers-Briggs Type Indicator (MBTI): Myers-Briggs类型指标（MBTI）是一种自省型自我调查报告，表明人们在对世界的看法和决策方式方面的心理偏好不同。该测试试图区分四种个性类别：内向或外向，感知或直觉，思维或感觉，判断或感知。

INFJs might seem timid when you first meet them, but don't be fooled by their quiet demeanor. They never shy away from a good challenge. Deep thinkers with rich inner lives, INFJs enjoy problem-solving and reflecting on ethics.

Six: They're classy AF!

This type likes the finer things in life. Whether it means enjoying a good glass of wine or wearing a snazzy pair of Oxfords, they strive for sophistication. It's important for them to look and feel good. You'll catch them owning one or two quality items instead of five cheap ones.

Seven: They make routine on boring.

INFJs are masters at organizing. From filing papers at work and color-coding bookshelves, to planning the week ahead with those nifty bullet journals. Meticulous about their details and regimens, you can always count on an INFJ to be prepared, punctual and persistent.

Are you an INFJ? Do you identify with these traits?

Key and sample answers

Viewing

Understanding the video clip

Facts about INFJS	The facts that impressed you	Reasons why the facts impressed you
1. They're magical unicorns!		Only one to two percent of the world's population are identified as INFJs.
2. They put the book in bookworm!		As introverts, INFJs love to pass time with the good old reading hour. They enjoy learning new things and have a broad range of interests.
3. They know how to climb the social ladder.		INFJs are ambitious, knowledge-seeking and always open to self-improvement.
4. They see things and understand them.		The minute they walk into a room they can absorb everyone's moods.
5. They love a good puzzle!		They never shy away from a good challenge. Deep thinkers with rich inner lives, INFJs enjoy problem-solving and reflecting on ethics.
6. They're classy AF!		INFJs like the finer things in life, and they would rather own one or two quality items instead of five cheap ones.
7. They make routine unboring.		INFJs are meticulous about their details and regimens, so they are always prepared, punctual and persistent.

Further thoughts

Cans	Can'ts
1. Read books together, whether it's history, Hogwarts or psychology.	1. Go to a party in a noisy bar together.
2. Struggle together to conquer the challenges in both study and life.	2. Keep complaining about life and do nothing to solve the problems.
3. Study people's mood if invited to a social gathering.	3. Just keep mind empty by dwelling in the crowd.
4. Enjoy a good-quality life like enjoying a good glass of wine.	4. Always buy cheap things.

Banked Cloze

1–5 BMIKG 6–10 OAHFD

Long Passage

1–5 DCBJI 6–10 FMHKL

Short Passages

Passage one 1–5: DABCC

Passage two 1–5: CCBAD

Reading Skills

Word	Prefix	Root	Suffix	Part of speech	Meaning
unacceptable	un	accept	able	adjective	not acceptable
participant		participate	ant	noun	people who participate in some activities
socialization		social	ization	noun	the action of establishing a socialist basis
finalize		final	ize	verb	make final, complete
inactivity	in	act	ivity	noun	the state of being inactive
adulthood		adult	hood	noun	the state of a person who has attained maturity

Academic Words in Use

1. appreciate   2. strategy   3. reluctant   4. pursue   5. maintain
6. focus   7. approach   8. estimated   9. participate   10. professional
11. challenged   12. motivate

Writing

Sample writing

Which Determines Your Personality, Genetics or Life Experience?

As some reports say, "The characteristics of us naturally have much more effect on our personality than other experience that we have in our life."

There is research suggesting that the characteristics we are born with have much more influence on our personality than any other experience we have in our life. Honestly, I agree with it.

It is our personal characteristics that decide what we will do when we face a situation and how we look at the world. Basically, our personality makes who we are and makes everyone a unique individual.

While personality influences us a lot, the experience we had still plays an important role in our life. Our experiences will definitely influence us, but the influence won't be as big as the characteristics we are born with. This is because our characteristics will decide how we think and this will result in different reactions and form different personalities.

In conclusion, it's important to know our personal characteristics so that we can make right decisions and choose a proper path of life for ourselves.

Unit 8   Let's Get Social

Building Social Connections

NW: 553   GL: 7.8   AWL percentage: 4.06 %   Duration: 3′03″   WPM: 181

Think of the last time you spent time with family, or friends, or people you care about. How did this make you feel?

Being connected with people in your life helps you feel like you belong. It even helps reduce stress, boost your immune system, lower blood pressure and can lengthen your life. In fact, people with strong social support are usually happier, have better mental health, and feel a stronger sense of belonging in their community.

Unfortunately, people who feel alone or isolated often have poor health. In fact, new research shows that not having social relationships can shorten our lives as much as smoking over 100 cigarettes per week. But the good news is that we can all do things to change this and to help ourselves and others feel more connected.

Let's look at an example. This is Sammy. He just moved to a new city and does not have any family there. Because his new job takes up a lot of his time, he hasn't made any close friends yet. He comes home from work most days and spends time by himself watching TV or on his computer. He misses having his family around and is starting to feel a little more sad and tired each day.

So what can Sammy do to get better connected with others? Sammy can start by getting out and exploring his new neighborhood. Maybe he can check out his community centre to see what activities they have there. He can have lunch or go for a walk with his new co-workers. Sammy loves cycling but doesn't know the area. He could visit a bike shop to see if there are neighborhood bike groups or look online for a bike group to join. Volunteering is another great way to get connected in your community. He could check out Volunteer Canada[1], the local newspaper or local agencies to see where volunteer help is needed.

Like most of us, there may be a time when Sammy needs a little more help. When moving to a new city, recovering from an illness or going through a life change, calling someone you trust or talking to a health professional can really help. If available, Sammy could get support from his employee assistance program or call 2-1-1[2] to find out about

---

1 Volunteer Canada: 加拿大国立义工组织，一家注册慈善机构，在志愿服务方面提供国家级别的领导和专业知识，以提高志愿人员体验的参与度、质量和多样性。

2 2-1-1: 在加拿大，2–1–1是提供社区信息和转介服务的专线号码，它是一个易于记忆且普遍被认可的数字，它将使需要帮助的个人和家庭与适当的基于社区的组织和政府机构之间建立关键的联系。

programs and resources for support. The reality is that we all need people in our life during good times and during tough times.

Make sure to reach out when you need help. Be open to accept help when it is offered and help others in return. So now, try to think about something you can do to make your connections stronger. Are there people in your life or groups that you could reach out to?

How about others in your community who would benefit from more connections? Could you offer to make a meal for a new parent or caregiver, or maybe a neighbor who is having a tough time? Write all of your ideas down and pick one thing you can do this week to get more connected or help others get more connected. Even small things like holding the door for someone, taking out the garbage for your neighbor, bringing food to someone in need.

These all can lead to big changes that can improve your connections, your physical health and your mental health.

Key and sample answers

Viewing

Understanding the video clip

Ways to get better connected with others	Mentioned
1. Get out and explore his new neighborhood.	√
2. Visit a bike shop to see if there are neighborhood bike groups.	√
3. Call 211 if you need a little more help.	√
4. Write your ideas down and pick one thing you can do for you neighbor.	√
5. Be open to accept help when it is offered and help others in return.	√
6. Go for a walk with your new co-workers.	√
7. Spend time by yourself watching TV or on your computer most of the days.	

Further thoughts

Benefits of building social connections
1. Building social connections can enhance your sense of happiness.
2. Building social connections can improve your health.

3. Building social connections can prolong your life span.
4. Building social connections can cultivate tenacity after experiencing hardships.
5. Building social connections can boost your immunity.
6. Building social connections will alleviate your anxiety.
7. Building social connections will enhance your self-esteem.

Banked Cloze

1–5 DHGCE   6–10 JAFBI

Long Passage

1–5 DLKBH   6–10 CJIGF

Short Passages

Passage one 1–5: BCACD
Passage two 1–5: ACBDA

Reading Skills

1–5: BACBD

Academic Words in Use

1. communicat   2. similar   3. established   4. media   5. network
6. researches   7. embarrassment 8. socially   9. comment   10. expert
11. display   12. joy

Sample writing

My Opinion on the Increasing Use of the Cell Phone

Cell phones are of great benefit to all of us. One of the most obvious advantages is that we can contact with our friends and relatives more conveniently than ever before. However, they are also the root that leads us to overuse them, which tends to exert a negative impact on our life. For example, overusing cell phones will reduce face-to-face communication among people. It seems that most of us enjoy the convenience of contact at the expense of reducing interpersonal communication. Moreover, a variety of social networking tools in mobile phones have occupied much of our time. Information distribution tools and social networking tools, in particular, have attracted all of our attention, which tempts us to keep our eyes on the screen almost every second. So, do not expect us to talk with the people around us—we don't have time!

To sum up, modern tools like cell phone should be served as an "angel" to improve our living standard, rather than a "devil" to disturb our normal life and interpersonal communication.